VB6CODE WARRIOR

Working with DAO

By Richard Thomas Edwards

CONTENTS

WELCOME TO DAO

The Godfather of Data Access

I CONSIDER DAO – which means Data Access Objects -TO BE THE GODFATHER OF DATA ACCESS BECAUSE IT HAS BEEN THE WAY TO CONNECT TO AND CREATE DATABASES, TABLES AND STORED PROCEEDURES YEARS BEFORE I WENT TO WORK FOR MICROSOFT.

In fact, knowing it helped me to land my first job at Microsoft.

But there was something coming through the development pipeline that made every attempt of dethroning it: Active X Data Objects.

Their reasoning was quite simple, Do the same thing in memory and it will be much faster.

Well, that worked until hard drives – SSDs and the newest kid on the block, USB SSDs – no longer made the speed distinction a factor and, once again, DAO is back in the spotlight.

LET'S VENTURE BACKWARDS IN TIME FOR JUST A MOMENT

Anyone who remembers the wild, wild Microsoft days knows what the worlds DLL HELL meant. Those were the good old days, right?

R.I.P to them!

Anyway, back then we had things like DAO.DBEngine.25–AKA the thunker – which served to support the notion that 16-bit and 32-bit versions of data access. It was Microsoft's way of appeasing the gods. And, of course that was short lived when

Microsoft grew up fast and started compromising quality support for higher profit margins.

So, by 1998, DAO.DBEngine.35, a 32-bit only Database Engine had been created and most us working in Technical Support were pretty sure ADO was going to replace it.

It didn't. In fact, when VB6 came out with DAO.DBEngine.36, we very quickly learned why.

In fact, I wrote two KB Articles on the issue. Then installation and the remove of Access 97 removed the key in the registry that made the VB6 development environment effectively useless with respect to DAO.

So, after that fiasco, most of us were pretty sure DAO was on the way out.

We were, once again, wrong.

Office 2007 shipped with DAO.DBEngine.120.

BACK TO THE FUTURE

Today, after installing Office 365, I find no changes in the COM version of DAO. The COM version supports dbVersion120. However, the .Net version of COM supports up to dbVersion150 according to the Object Browser. I'm not even sure that is possible considering the same functionality found in the .Net COM version should be the same.

For right now, none of this really matters as we need to focus on connecting to DAO and what you can do with what you have installed.

WHAT DAO CAN DO FOR YOU

First, DAO supports local as well as remote connections.

Second, you can connect to a database using:

There are ISAMS -- Indexed Sequential Access Method – well as all the ODBC – Open Database Connectivity – drivers including SQL Server that can be used along with the standard connectivity using database naming. Below are some examples of what is meant:

STANDARD DATABASE CONNECTION

Please keep in mind that you could use DAO.DBEngine.35, DAO.DBEngine.36 or DAO.DBEngine.120 with all the below examples.

```
Dim Filename
Filename = "C:\Program Files (x86)\Microsoft Visual Studio\VB98\Nwind.mdb"
Set DBEngine = CreateObject("DAO.DBEngine.36")
Set db = DBEngine.OpenDatabase(filename)
```

A ISAM CONNECTION USING DAO

It works like this:

```
Filename = "C:\ISAMS\Text"
Set DBEngine = CreateObject("DAO.DBEngine.36")
Set db = DBEngine.OpenDatabase(filename, , , "Text; hdr=yes;")
```

And the Query:
```
Set rs = db.OpenRecordset("Select * from [Myfile.csv]")
```

TO CREATE A DAO DATABASE

```
dbLangGeneral = ";LANGID=0x0409;CP=1252;COUNTRY=0"

dbVersion30 = 32
dbVersion40 = 64
dbVersion120 = 128

Set dbEngine = CreateObject("DAO.DBEngine.120")
Set db = dbEngine.CreateDatabase("C:\MyFirst.accdb", dbLangGeneral, dbVersion120)

Set dbEngine = CreateObject("DAO.DBEngine.36")
```

```
Set    db    =    dbEngine.CreateDatabase("C:\MyFirst.mdb",    dbLangGeneral,
dbVersion40)

Set dbEngine = CreateObject("DAO.DBEngine.35")
Set    db    =    dbEngine.CreateDatabase("C:\MyFirst.mdb",    dbLangGeneral,
dbVersion30)
```

TO OPEN THE DATABASE

```
Set dbEngine = CreateObject("DAO.DBEngine.120")
Set db = dbEngine.OpenDatabase("C:\MyFirst.accdb")

Set dbEngine = CreateObject("DAO.DBEngine.36")
Set db = dbEngine.OpenDatabase("C:\MyFirst.mdb")

Set dbEngine = CreateObject("DAO.DBEngine.35")
Set db = dbEngine.OpenDatabase("C:\MyFirst.mdb")
```

CREATE AND POPULATE TABLE

```
Set tbldef = db.CreateTableDef("Process_Properties")
For x = 0 To rs1. Fields.Count-1
  fld = tbldef.CreateField(Prop.Name, 12)
  fld.AllowZeroLength = true
  tbldef.Fields.Append(fld)
Next
db.TableDefs.Append(tbldef)
```

I use 12 or a memo field because I don't want to have to worry about the data type or the size of the information I'm passing in. This could become problematic if I didn't.

```
Set rs = db.OpenRecordset("Processes_Properties")
Do While rs1.EOF = false
  rs.AddNew()
  for x = 0 to rs1.Fields.Count-1
    rs.Fields[x].Value = str(rs1.Fields[x].Value)
  Next
  rs.Update()
  rs1.MoveFirst()
Loop
```

```
Set rs = db.OpenRecordset("Select * From Processes_Properties",
Exclusive:=False)
```

Or:

```
Set rs = db.OpenRecordset("Processes_Properties")
```

TABLES AND VIEWS

At this point you're probably scratching your head trying to figure out how I went from creating a query against a known table. Well, in DAO, it can't get much easier than this:

```
Set DBEngine = CreateObject("DAO.DBEngine.36")
Set db = DBEngine.OpenDatabase("D:\NWind.mdb")

For each tbldef in db.TableDefs
    If mid(tbldef.Name, 1, 4) <> "MSys" then
        WScript.Echo(tbldef.Name)
    End If
Next
```

The Results:

Categories
Customers
Employees
Order Details
Orders
Products
Shippers
Suppliers

As for Views:

```
Set DBEngine = CreateObject("DAO.DBEngine.36")
Set db = DBEngine.OpenDatabase("D:\NWind.mdb")

For each QDef in db.QueryDefs
    WScript.Echo(tbldef.Name)
Next
```

The Results:

Category Sales for 1995
Current Product List
Invoices
Order Details Extended
Order Subtotals
Product Sales for 1995
Products Above Average Price
Quarterly Orders
Sales by Category
Ten Most Expensive Products

Okay, so now you know something about connection strings and how to get table and view information, it is time to start using that information to create an assortment of user outputs which just might make you and your boss get some warm and fuzzy feelings.

ASP CODE

THERE IS NOTING FANTASIC ABOUT CREATING ASP OR ASPX WEB PAGES. In fact, additional hoops must be jumped - web site where you can cut and paste what you just created from here is one of them. So, with that said, I've added enough bells and whistles into the code structure to make it worth your while. Here's what is in store for you:

- Report View
    - Horizontal
        - None
        - Button
        - Combobox
        - Div
        - Link
        - Listbox
        - Span
        - Textarea
        - Textbox
    - Vertical
        - None
        - Button
        - Combobox
        - Div
        - Link

- Listbox
- Span
- Textarea
- Textbox

- Table View
  - Horizontal
    - None
    - Button
    - Combobox
    - Div
    - Link
    - Listbox
    - Span
    - Textarea
    - Textbox
  - Vertical
    - None
    - Button
    - Combobox
    - Div
    - Link
    - Listbox
    - Span
    - Textarea
    - Textbox

```
Set ws = CreateObject("WScript.Shell")
Set fso = CreateObject("Scripting.FileSystemObject")
Set txtstream =fso.OpenTextFile(ws.CurrentDirectory + "\Products.asp", 2, true,
-2)
    txtstream.WriteLine("<html>")
    txtstream.WriteLine("<head>")
    txtstream.WriteLine("<title>" + Tablename + "</title>")
    #Add Stylesheet here
    txtstream.WriteLine("<body>")
    txtstream.WriteLine("</br>")
```

Horizontal Reports

```
    txtstream.WriteLine("<table border=0 cellspacing=3 cellpadding=3>")
    txtstream.WriteLine("<%")
    txtstream.WriteLine("Response.Write(""<tr>""" + vbcrlf)")
    For x = 0 to rs.Fields.Count-1
        txtstream.WriteLine("Response.Write(""<th    style=""   font-family:Calibri,
Sans-Serif;font-size:  12px;color:darkred;""" align='left'  nowrap='nowrap'>" +
rs.Fields(x).Name + "</th>""" + vbcrlf)")
    Next
    txtstream.WriteLine("Response.Write(""</tr>""" + vbcrlf)")
    Do While(rs.EOF = false)
        txtstream.WriteLine("Response.Write(""<tr>""" + vbcrlf)")
        For x = 0 to rs.Fields.Count-1
```

NONE

```
        txtstream.WriteLine("Response.Write(""<td   style=""""font-family:Calibri,
Sans-Serif;font-size:  12px;color:navy;""" align='left'  nowrap='nowrap'>"   +
rs.Fields(x).Value + "</td>""" + vbcrlf)")
```

Button

```
txtstream.WriteLine("Response.Write("""<td   style="""font-family:Calibri,
Sans-Serif;font-size:  12px;color:navy;"""   align='left'   nowrap='true'><button
style='width:100%;' value ="' + rs.Fields(x).Value + "'>" + rs.Fields(x).Value +
"</button></td>""" + vbcrlf)")
```

COMBOBOX

```
txtstream.WriteLine("Response.Write("""<td   style="""font-family:Calibri,
Sans-Serif;font-size: 12px;color:navy;""" align='left' nowrap='true'><select><option
value   =   """   +   rs.Fields(x).Value   +   """>"   +   rs.Fields(x).Value   +
"</option></select></td>""" + vbcrlf)")
```

DIV

```
txtstream.WriteLine("Response.Write("""<td   style="""font-family:Calibri,
Sans-Serif;font-size:  12px;color:navy;"""  align='left'  nowrap='true'><div>"  +
rs.Fields(x).Value + "</div></td>""" + vbcrlf)")
```

LINK

```
txtstream.WriteLine("Response.Write("""<td   style="""font-family:Calibri,
Sans-Serif;font-size: 12px;color:navy;""" align='left' nowrap='true'><a href='" +
rs.Fields(x).Value + "'>" + rs.Fields(x).Value + "</a></td>""" + vbcrlf)")
```

LISTBOX

```
txtstream.WriteLine("Response.Write("""<td   style="""font-family:Calibri,
Sans-Serif;font-size:   12px;color:navy;"""   align='left'   nowrap='true'><select
multiple><option value = """ + rs.Fields(x).Value + """>" + rs.Fields(x).Value +
"</option></select></td>""" + vbcrlf)")
```

SPAN

```
txtstream.WriteLine("Response.Write("""<td   style="""font-family:Calibri,
Sans-Serif;font-size:  12px;color:navy;"""  align='left'  nowrap='true'><span>"  +
rs.Fields(x).Value + "</span></td>""" + vbcrlf)")
```

TEXTAREA

```
        txtstream.WriteLine("Response.Write(""<td  style=""font-family:Calibri,
Sans-Serif;font-size: 12px;color:navy;"" align='left' nowrap='true'><textarea>" +
rs.Fields(x).Value + "</textarea></td>""" + vbcrlf)")
```

TEXTBOX

```
        txtstream.WriteLine("Response.Write(""<td  style=""font-family:Calibri,
Sans-Serif;font-size:   12px;color:navy;""   align='left'   nowrap='true'><input
type=text value=""""" + rs.Fields(x).Value + """""></input></td>""" + vbcrlf)")
        Next
        txtstream.WriteLine("Response.Write(""</tr>""" + vbcrlf)")
        rs.MoveNext
    Loop
    txtstream.WriteLine("%>")
    txtstream.WriteLine("</table>")
    txtstream.WriteLine("</body>")
    txtstream.WriteLine("</html>")
    txtstream.Close()
```

Vertical Reports

```
    txtstream.WriteLine("<table border=0 cellspacing=3 cellpadding=3>")
    txtstream.WriteLine("<%")
    For x = 0 to rs.Fields.Count-1
        txtstream.WriteLine("Response.Write(""<tr><th         style=""    font-
family:Calibri,    Sans-Serif;font-size:    12px;color:darkred;""    align='left'
nowrap='nowrap'>" + rs.Fields(x).Name + "</th>""" + vbcrlf)")
        rs.MoveFirst()
        Do While(rs.EOF = false)
        txtstream.WriteLine("Response.Write(""<td  style=""font-family:Calibri,
Sans-Serif;font-size: 12px;color:navy;"">"  +  rs.Fields(x).Value  +  "</td>"""  +
vbcrlf)")
```

NONE

```
        txtstream.WriteLine("Response.Write(""<td  style=""font-family:Calibri,
Sans-Serif;font-size:  12px;color:navy;""  align='left'  nowrap='nowrap'>"   +
rs.Fields(x).Value + "</td>""" + vbcrlf)")
```

Button

```
        txtstream.WriteLine("Response.Write(""""<td    style=""""font-family:Calibri,
Sans-Serif;font-size:  12px;color:navy;""""  align='left'  nowrap='true'><button
style='width:100%;' value ='" + rs.Fields(x).Value + "'>" + rs.Fields(x).Value +
"</button></td>"""" + vbcrlf)")
```

Combobox

```
        txtstream.WriteLine("Response.Write(""""<td    style=""""font-family:Calibri,
Sans-Serif;font-size: 12px;color:navy;"""" align='left' nowrap='true'><select><option
value   =   """"""   +   rs.Fields(x).Value   +   """""">"   +   rs.Fields(x).Value   +
"</option></select></td>"""" + vbcrlf)")
```

Div

```
        txtstream.WriteLine("Response.Write(""""<td    style=""""font-family:Calibri,
Sans-Serif;font-size:  12px;color:navy;""""  align='left'  nowrap='true'><div>"   +
rs.Fields(x).Value + "</div></td>"""" + vbcrlf)")
```

Link

```
        txtstream.WriteLine("Response.Write(""""<td style=""""font-family:Calibri, Sans-
Serif;font-size:  12px;color:navy;""""  align='left'  nowrap='true'><a href='"   +
rs.Fields(x).Value + "'>" + rs.Fields(x).Value + "</a></td>"""" + vbcrlf)")
```

Listbox

```
        txtstream.WriteLine("Response.Write(""""<td style=""""font-family:Calibri, Sans-
Serif;font-size:    12px;color:navy;""""    align='left'    nowrap='true'><select
multiple><option value = """""" + rs.Fields(x).Value + """""">" + rs.Fields(x).Value +
"</option></select></td>"""" + vbcrlf)")
```

Span

```
txtstream.WriteLine("Response.Write(""<td        style="""font-family:Calibri,
Sans-Serif;font-size: 12px;color:navy;""" align='left' nowrap='true'><span>" +
rs.Fields(x).Value + "</span></td>""" + vbcrlf)")
```

Textarea

```
txtstream.WriteLine("Response.Write(""<td style="""font-family:Calibri, Sans-
Serif;font-size:  12px;color:navy;"""  align='left'  nowrap='true'><textarea>"  +
rs.Fields(x).Value + "</textarea></td>""" + vbcrlf)")
```

Textbox

```
        txtstream.WriteLine("Response.Write(""<td        style="""font-family:Calibri,
Sans-Serif;font-size:     12px;color:navy;"""     align='left'     nowrap='true'><input
type=text value="""" + rs.Fields(x).Value + """"></input></td>""" + vbcrlf)")
        rs.MoveNext
        loop
        txtstream.WriteLine("Response.Write(""</tr>""" + vbcrlf)")
Next
txtstream.WriteLine("%>")
txtstream.WriteLine("</table>")
txtstream.WriteLine("</body>")
txtstream.WriteLine("</html>")
txtstream.Close()
```

Horizontal Tables

```
txtstream.WriteLine("<table        style='border:Double;border-width:1px;border-
color:navy;' rules=all frames=both cellpadding=2 cellspacing=2 Width=0>")
        txtstream.WriteLine("<%")
        txtstream.WriteLine("Response.Write(""<tr>""" + vbcrlf)")
        For x = 0 to rs.Fields.Count-1
        txtstream.WriteLine("Response.Write(""<th        style="""       font-family:Calibri,
Sans-Serif;font-size:  12px;color:darkred;"""  align='left'  nowrap='nowrap'>"  +
rs.Fields(x).Name + "</th>""" + vbcrlf)")

        Next
```

```
   txtstream.WriteLine("Response.Write(""</tr>"" + vbcrlf)")
   Do While(rs.EOF = false)
     txtstream.WriteLine("Response.Write(""<tr>"" + vbcrlf)")
       For x = 0 to rs.Fields.Count-1
```

NONE

```
        txtstream.WriteLine("Response.Write(""<td  style=""font-family:Calibri,
Sans-Serif;font-size:  12px;color:navy;""  align='left'  nowrap='nowrap'>"  +
rs.Fields(x).Value + "</td>"" + vbcrlf)")
```

Button

```
        txtstream.WriteLine("Response.Write(""<td  style=""font-family:Calibri,
Sans-Serif;font-size:  12px;color:navy;""  align='left'  nowrap='true'><button
style='width:100%;' value ='" + rs.Fields(x).Value + "'>" + rs.Fields(x).Value +
"</button></td>"" + vbcrlf)")
```

COMBOBOX

```
        txtstream.WriteLine("Response.Write(""<td   style=""font-family:Calibri,
Sans-Serif;font-size: 12px;color:navy;"" align='left' nowrap='true'><select><option
value   =   """   +   rs.Fields(x).Value   +   """>"   +   rs.Fields(x).Value   +
"</option></select></td>"" + vbcrlf)")
```

DIV

```
        txtstream.WriteLine("Response.Write(""<td   style=""font-family:Calibri,
Sans-Serif;font-size:  12px;color:navy;""  align='left'  nowrap='true'><div>"  +
rs.Fields(x).Value + "</div></td>"" + vbcrlf)")
```

LINK

```
        txtstream.WriteLine("Response.Write(""<td   style=""font-family:Calibri,
Sans-Serif;font-size: 12px;color:navy;"" align='left' nowrap='true'><a href='" +
rs.Fields(x).Value + "'>" + rs.Fields(x).Value + "</a></td>"" + vbcrlf)")
```

LISTBOX

```
        txtstream.WriteLine("Response.Write(""<td   style=""font-family:Calibri,
Sans-Serif;font-size:   12px;color:navy;""   align='left'   nowrap='true'><select
multiple><option value = """ + rs.Fields(x).Value + """>" + rs.Fields(x).Value +
"</option></select></td>""" + vbcrlf)")
```

SPAN

```
        txtstream.WriteLine("Response.Write(""<td   style=""font-family:Calibri,
Sans-Serif;font-size:  12px;color:navy;""  align='left'  nowrap='true'><span>" +
rs.Fields(x).Value + "</span></td>""" + vbcrlf)")
```

TEXTAREA

```
        txtstream.WriteLine("Response.Write(""<td   style=""font-family:Calibri,
Sans-Serif;font-size: 12px;color:navy;""  align='left' nowrap='true'><textarea>" +
rs.Fields(x).Value + "</textarea></td>""" + vbcrlf)")
```

TEXTBOX

```
        txtstream.WriteLine("Response.Write(""<td   style=""font-family:Calibri,
Sans-Serif;font-size:   12px;color:navy;""   align='left'   nowrap='true'><input
type=text value=""" + rs.Fields(x).Value + """></input></td>""" + vbcrlf)")

        txtstream.WriteLine("Response.Write(""</tr>""" + vbcrlf)")
        rs.MoveNext

    txtstream.WriteLine("%>")
    txtstream.WriteLine("</table>")
    txtstream.WriteLine("</body>")
    txtstream.WriteLine("</html>")
    txtstream.Close()
```

Vertical Tables

```
    txtstream.WriteLine("<table       style='border:Double;border-width:1px;border-
color:navy;' rules=all frames=both cellpadding=2 cellspacing=2 Width=0>")
```

```
txtstream.WriteLine("<%")

For x = 0 to rs.Fields.Count-1
        txtstream.WriteLine("Response.Write("""<tr><th         style=""      font-
family:Calibri,      Sans-Serif;font-size:      12px;color:darkred;"""      align='left'
nowrap='nowrap'>" + rs.Fields(x).Name + "</th>""" + vbcrlf)")
        rs.MoveFirst()
        Do While(rs.EOF = false)
        txtstream.WriteLine("Response.Write("""<td     style=""font-family:Calibri,
Sans-Serif;font-size:  12px;color:navy;""">" + rs.Fields(x).Value + "</td>""" +
vbcrlf)")
```

NONE

```
        txtstream.WriteLine("Response.Write("""<td  style=""font-family:Calibri,
Sans-Serif;font-size:  12px;color:navy;"""  align='left'  nowrap='nowrap'>"  +
rs.Fields(x).Value + "</td>""" + vbcrlf)")
```

Button

```
        txtstream.WriteLine("Response.Write("""<td     style=""font-family:Calibri,
Sans-Serif;font-size:   12px;color:navy;"""   align='left'   nowrap='true'><button
style='width:100%;' value ='" + rs.Fields(x).Value + "'>" + rs.Fields(x).Value +
"</button></td>""" + vbcrlf)")
```

Combobox

```
        txtstream.WriteLine("Response.Write("""<td    style=""font-family:Calibri,
Sans-Serif;font-size: 12px;color:navy;""" align='left' nowrap='true'><select><option
value   =   """   +   rs.Fields(x).Value   +   """">"   +   rs.Fields(x).Value   +
"</option></select></td>""" + vbcrlf)")
```

Div

```
        txtstream.WriteLine("Response.Write("""<td     style=""font-family:Calibri,
Sans-Serif;font-size:  12px;color:navy;"""  align='left'  nowrap='true'><div>"  +
rs.Fields(x).Value + "</div></td>""" + vbcrlf)")
```

Link

```
txtstream.WriteLine("Response.Write(""<td style=""font-family:Calibri, Sans-Serif;font-size: 12px;color:navy;"" align='left' nowrap='true'><a href='" + rs.Fields(x).Value + "'>" + rs.Fields(x).Value + "</a></td>"" + vbcrlf)")
```

Listbox

```
txtstream.WriteLine("Response.Write(""<td style=""font-family:Calibri, Sans-Serif;font-size: 12px;color:navy;"" align='left' nowrap='true'><select multiple><option value = """ + rs.Fields(x).Value + """>" + rs.Fields(x).Value + "</option></select></td>"" + vbcrlf)")
```

Span

```
txtstream.WriteLine("Response.Write(""<td style=""font-family:Calibri, Sans-Serif;font-size: 12px;color:navy;"" align='left' nowrap='true'><span>" + rs.Fields(x).Value + "</span></td>"" + vbcrlf)")
```

Textarea

```
txtstream.WriteLine("Response.Write(""<td style=""font-family:Calibri, Sans-Serif;font-size: 12px;color:navy;"" align='left' nowrap='true'><textarea>" + rs.Fields(x).Value + "</textarea></td>"" + vbcrlf)")
```

Textbox

```
txtstream.WriteLine("Response.Write(""<td style=""font-family:Calibri, Sans-Serif;font-size: 12px;color:navy;"" align='left' nowrap='true'><input type=text value=""" + rs.Fields(x).Value + """></input></td>"" + vbcrlf)")
    rs.MoveNext

txtstream.WriteLine("Response.Write(""</tr>"" + vbcrlf)")

txtstream.WriteLine("%>")
txtstream.WriteLine("</table>")
txtstream.WriteLine("</body>")
```

```
txtstream.WriteLine("</html>")
txtstream.Close()
```

ASPX CODE

B ELOW ARE EXAMPLES OF USING ADO THROUGH VBSCRIPT TO CREATE ASPX FILES.

```
Set ws = CreateObject("WScript.Shell")
Set fso = CreateObject("Scripting.FileSystemObject")
Set txtstream =fso.OpenTextFile(ws.CurrentDirectory + "\Products.asp", 2, true,
-2)
    txtstream.WriteLine("<html>")
    txtstream.WriteLine("<head>")
    txtstream.WriteLine("<title>" + Tablename + "</title>")
    #Add Stylesheet here
    txtstream.WriteLine("<body>")
    txtstream.WriteLine("</br>")
```

Horizontal Reports

```
    txtstream.WriteLine("<table border=0 cellspacing=3 cellpadding=3>")
    txtstream.WriteLine("<%")
    txtstream.WriteLine("Response.Write(""<tr>""" + vbcrlf)")
    For x = 0 to rs.Fields.Count-1
        txtstream.WriteLine("Response.Write(""<th     style=""   font-family:Calibri,
Sans-Serif;font-size:  12px;color:darkred;""" align='left'  nowrap='nowrap'>" +
rs.Fields(x).Name + "</th>""" + vbcrlf)")
    Next
```

```vb
txtstream.WriteLine("Response.Write(""</tr>""" + vbcrlf)")
Do While(rs.EOF = false)
  txtstream.WriteLine("Response.Write(""<tr>""" + vbcrlf)")
  For x = 0 to rs.Fields.Count-1
```

NONE

```vb
        txtstream.WriteLine("Response.Write(""<td    style=""""font-family:Calibri,
Sans-Serif;font-size:   12px;color:navy;""""    align='left'    nowrap='nowrap'>" +
rs.Fields(x).Value + "</td>""" + vbcrlf)")
```

Button

```vb
        txtstream.WriteLine("Response.Write(""<td    style=""""font-family:Calibri,
Sans-Serif;font-size:   12px;color:navy;""""    align='left'    nowrap='true'><button
style='width:100%;' value ='" + rs.Fields(x).Value + "'>" + rs.Fields(x).Value +
"</button></td>""" + vbcrlf)")
```

COMBOBOX

```vb
        txtstream.WriteLine("Response.Write(""<td    style=""""font-family:Calibri,
Sans-Serif;font-size: 12px;color:navy;"""" align='left' nowrap='true'><select><option
value   =   """"   +   rs.Fields(x).Value   +   """">"   +   rs.Fields(x).Value   +
"</option></select></td>""" + vbcrlf)")
```

DIV

```vb
        txtstream.WriteLine("Response.Write(""<td    style=""""font-family:Calibri,
Sans-Serif;font-size:   12px;color:navy;""""    align='left'    nowrap='true'><div>" +
rs.Fields(x).Value + "</div></td>""" + vbcrlf)")
```

LINK

```vb
        txtstream.WriteLine("Response.Write(""<td    style=""""font-family:Calibri,
Sans-Serif;font-size: 12px;color:navy;"""" align='left' nowrap='true'><a href='" +
rs.Fields(x).Value + "'>" + rs.Fields(x).Value + "</a></td>""" + vbcrlf)")
```

LISTBOX

```
        txtstream.WriteLine("Response.Write(""<td   style="""font-family:Calibri,
Sans-Serif;font-size:  12px;color:navy;"""   align='left'  nowrap='true'><select
multiple><option value = """ + rs.Fields(x).Value + """>" + rs.Fields(x).Value +
"</option></select></td>""" + vbcrlf)")
```

SPAN

```
        txtstream.WriteLine("Response.Write(""<td   style="""font-family:Calibri,
Sans-Serif;font-size:  12px;color:navy;"""  align='left'  nowrap='true'><span>"  +
rs.Fields(x).Value + "</span></td>""" + vbcrlf)")
```

TEXTAREA

```
        txtstream.WriteLine("Response.Write(""<td   style="""font-family:Calibri,
Sans-Serif;font-size: 12px;color:navy;"""  align='left' nowrap='true'><textarea>"  +
rs.Fields(x).Value + "</textarea></td>""" + vbcrlf)")
```

TEXTBOX

```
        txtstream.WriteLine("Response.Write(""<td   style="""font-family:Calibri,
Sans-Serif;font-size:  12px;color:navy;"""   align='left'   nowrap='true'><input
type=text value="""" + rs.Fields(x).Value + """"></input></td>""" + vbcrlf)")

    Next
    txtstream.WriteLine("Response.Write(""</tr>""" + vbcrlf)")
    rs.MoveNext
Loop
txtstream.WriteLine("%>")
txtstream.WriteLine("</table>")
txtstream.WriteLine("</body>")
txtstream.WriteLine("</html>")
txtstream.Close()
```

Vertical Reports

```
txtstream.WriteLine("<table border=0 cellspacing=3 cellpadding=3>")
txtstream.WriteLine("<%")
For x = 0 to rs.Fields.Count-1
      txtstream.WriteLine("Response.Write(""<tr><th          style=""    font-
family:Calibri,      Sans-Serif;font-size:      12px;color:darkred;""       align='left'
nowrap='nowrap'>" + rs.Fields(x).Name + "</th>""" + vbcrlf)")
      rs.MoveFirst()
      Do While(rs.EOF = false)
       txtstream.WriteLine("Response.Write(""<td   style=""""font-family:Calibri,
Sans-Serif;font-size:   12px;color:navy;"">" + rs.Fields(x).Value + "</td>""" +
vbcrlf)")
```

NONE

```
        txtstream.WriteLine("Response.Write(""<td style=""""font-family:Calibri,
Sans-Serif;font-size:   12px;color:navy;""    align='left'   nowrap='nowrap'>"   +
rs.Fields(x).Value + "</td>""" + vbcrlf)")
```

Button

```
        txtstream.WriteLine("Response.Write(""<td    style=""""font-family:Calibri,
Sans-Serif;font-size:    12px;color:navy;""     align='left'    nowrap='true'><button
style='width:100%;' value ='" + rs.Fields(x).Value + "'>" + rs.Fields(x).Value +
"</button></td>""" + vbcrlf)")
```

Combobox

```
        txtstream.WriteLine("Response.Write(""<td     style=""""font-family:Calibri,
Sans-Serif;font-size: 12px;color:navy;"" align='left' nowrap='true'><select><option
value   =    """    +    rs.Fields(x).Value    +    """">"    +    rs.Fields(x).Value    +
"</option></select></td>""" + vbcrlf)")
```

Div

```
        txtstream.WriteLine("Response.Write(""<td      style=""""font-family:Calibri,
Sans-Serif;font-size:   12px;color:navy;""    align='left'   nowrap='true'><div>"   +
rs.Fields(x).Value + "</div></td>""" + vbcrlf)")
```

Link

txtstream.WriteLine("Response.Write(""<td style=""font-family:Calibri, Sans-Serif;font-size: 12px;color:navy;"" align='left' nowrap='true'><a href='" + rs.Fields(x).Value + "'>" + rs.Fields(x).Value + "</a></td>"" + vbcrlf)")

Listbox

txtstream.WriteLine("Response.Write(""<td style=""font-family:Calibri, Sans-Serif;font-size: 12px;color:navy;"" align='left' nowrap='true'><select multiple><option value = """ + rs.Fields(x).Value + """>" + rs.Fields(x).Value + "</option></select></td>"" + vbcrlf)")

Span

txtstream.WriteLine("Response.Write(""<td style=""font-family:Calibri, Sans-Serif;font-size: 12px;color:navy;"" align='left' nowrap='true'>" + rs.Fields(x).Value + "</td>"" + vbcrlf)")

Textarea

txtstream.WriteLine("Response.Write(""<td style=""font-family:Calibri, Sans-Serif;font-size: 12px;color:navy;"" align='left' nowrap='true'><textarea>" + rs.Fields(x).Value + "</textarea></td>"" + vbcrlf)")

Textbox

txtstream.WriteLine("Response.Write(""<td style=""font-family:Calibri, Sans-Serif;font-size: 12px;color:navy;"" align='left' nowrap='true'><input type=text value=""" + rs.Fields(x).Value + """></input></td>"" + vbcrlf)")
        rs.MoveNext
      Loop
    txtstream.WriteLine("Response.Write(""</tr>"" + vbcrlf)")
  Next
  txtstream.WriteLine("%>")
  txtstream.WriteLine("</table>")
  txtstream.WriteLine("</body>")
  txtstream.WriteLine("</html>")

```
    txtstream.Close()
```

Horizontal Tables

```
    txtstream.WriteLine("<table          style='border:Double;border-width:1px;border-
color:navy;' rules=all frames=both cellpadding=2 cellspacing=2 Width=0>")
    txtstream.WriteLine("<%")
    txtstream.WriteLine("Response.Write(""<tr>""" + vbcrlf)")
    For x = 0 to rs.Fields.Count-1
      txtstream.WriteLine("Response.Write(""<th    style=""    font-family:Calibri,
Sans-Serif;font-size:  12px;color:darkred;""    align='left'    nowrap='nowrap'>"   +
rs.Fields(x).Name + "</th>""" + vbcrlf)")
    Next
    txtstream.WriteLine("Response.Write(""</tr>""" + vbcrlf)")
    Do While(rs.EOF = false)
      txtstream.WriteLine("Response.Write(""<tr>""" + vbcrlf)")
        For x = 0 to rs.Fields.Count-1
```

NONE

```
          txtstream.WriteLine("Response.Write(""<td   style=""""font-family:Calibri,
Sans-Serif;font-size:   12px;color:navy;""""   align='left'   nowrap='nowrap'>"   +
rs.Fields(x).Value + "</td>""" + vbcrlf)")
```

Button

```
          txtstream.WriteLine("Response.Write(""<td   style=""""font-family:Calibri,
Sans-Serif;font-size:  12px;color:navy;""""    align='left'   nowrap='true'><button
style='width:100%;' value ="" + rs.Fields(x).Value + "'>" + rs.Fields(x).Value +
"</button></td>""" + vbcrlf)")
```

COMBOBOX

```
          txtstream.WriteLine("Response.Write(""<td   style=""""font-family:Calibri,
Sans-Serif;font-size: 12px;color:navy;"""" align='left' nowrap='true'><select><option
```

```
value  =  """"  +  rs.Fields(x).Value  +  """">"  +  rs.Fields(x).Value  +
"</option></select></td>""" + vbcrlf)")
```

DIV

```
        txtstream.WriteLine("Response.Write(""<td  style=""font-family:Calibri,
Sans-Serif;font-size:  12px;color:navy;""  align='left'  nowrap='true'><div>"  +
rs.Fields(x).Value + "</div></td>""" + vbcrlf)")
```

LINK

```
        txtstream.WriteLine("Response.Write(""<td  style=""font-family:Calibri,
Sans-Serif;font-size: 12px;color:navy;""  align='left' nowrap='true'><a href='" +
rs.Fields(x).Value + "'>" + rs.Fields(x).Value + "</a></td>""" + vbcrlf)")
```

LISTBOX

```
        txtstream.WriteLine("Response.Write(""<td  style=""font-family:Calibri,
Sans-Serif;font-size:  12px;color:navy;""   align='left'   nowrap='true'><select
multiple><option value = """" + rs.Fields(x).Value + """">" + rs.Fields(x).Value +
"</option></select></td>""" + vbcrlf)")
```

SPAN

```
        txtstream.WriteLine("Response.Write(""<td  style=""font-family:Calibri,
Sans-Serif;font-size: 12px;color:navy;""  align='left'  nowrap='true'><span>"  +
rs.Fields(x).Value + "</span></td>""" + vbcrlf)")
```

TEXTAREA

```
        txtstream.WriteLine("Response.Write(""<td  style=""font-family:Calibri,
Sans-Serif;font-size: 12px;color:navy;"" align='left' nowrap='true'><textarea>" +
rs.Fields(x).Value + "</textarea></td>""" + vbcrlf)")
```

TEXTBOX

```
        txtstream.WriteLine("Response.Write(""<td  style=""font-family:Calibri,
Sans-Serif;font-size:   12px;color:navy;""    align='left'    nowrap='true'><input
type=text value="""" + rs.Fields(x).Value + """"></input></td>""" + vbcrlf)")
        Next
```

```
        txtstream.WriteLine("Response.Write(""</tr>""" + vbcrlf)")
        rs.MoveNext
Loop
txtstream.WriteLine("%>")
txtstream.WriteLine("</table>")
txtstream.WriteLine("</body>")
txtstream.WriteLine("</html>")
txtstream.Close()
```

Vertical Tables

```
txtstream.WriteLine("<table        style='border:Double;border-width:1px;border-
color:navy;' rules=all frames=both cellpadding=2 cellspacing=2 Width=0>")
txtstream.WriteLine("<%")
For x = 0 to rs.Fields.Count-1
        txtstream.WriteLine("Response.Write(""<tr><th        style=""        font-
family:Calibri,    Sans-Serif;font-size:    12px;color:darkred;""    align='left'
nowrap='nowrap'>" + rs.Fields(x).Name + "</th>""" + vbcrlf)")
        rs.MoveFirst()
        Do While rs.EOF = false
        txtstream.WriteLine("Response.Write(""<td    style=""font-family:Calibri,
Sans-Serif;font-size:  12px;color:navy;"">" + rs.Fields(x).Value + "</td>""" +
vbcrlf)")
```

NONE

```
        txtstream.WriteLine("Response.Write(""<td  style=""font-family:Calibri,
Sans-Serif;font-size:  12px;color:navy;""  align='left'  nowrap='nowrap'>" +
rs.Fields(x).Value + "</td>""" + vbcrlf)")
```

Button

```
        txtstream.WriteLine("Response.Write(""<td    style=""font-family:Calibri,
Sans-Serif;font-size:  12px;color:navy;""  align='left'  nowrap='true'><button
style='width:100%;' value ='" + rs.Fields(x).Value + "'>" + rs.Fields(x).Value +
"</button></td>""" + vbcrlf)")
```

Combobox

```
txtstream.WriteLine("Response.Write("""<td    style=""""font-family:Calibri,
Sans-Serif;font-size: 12px;color:navy;"""" align='left' nowrap='true'><select><option
value =  """" + rs.Fields(x).Value + """"">" + rs.Fields(x).Value +
"</option></select></td>"""" + vbcrlf)")
```

Div

```
txtstream.WriteLine("Response.Write("""<td    style=""""font-family:Calibri,
Sans-Serif;font-size: 12px;color:navy;""""  align='left'  nowrap='true'><div>"  +
rs.Fields(x).Value + "</div></td>"""" + vbcrlf)")
```

Link

```
txtstream.WriteLine("Response.Write("""<td style=""""font-family:Calibri, Sans-
Serif;font-size: 12px;color:navy;""""  align='left'  nowrap='true'><a  href='"  +
rs.Fields(x).Value + "'>" + rs.Fields(x).Value + "</a></td>"""" + vbcrlf)")
```

Listbox

```
txtstream.WriteLine("Response.Write("""<td style=""""font-family:Calibri, Sans-
Serif;font-size:  12px;color:navy;""""    align='left'    nowrap='true'><select
multiple><option value = """" + rs.Fields(x).Value + """"">" + rs.Fields(x).Value +
"</option></select></td>"""" + vbcrlf)")
```

Span

```
txtstream.WriteLine("Response.Write("""<td    style=""""font-family:Calibri,
Sans-Serif;font-size: 12px;color:navy;"""" align='left' nowrap='true'><span>" +
rs.Fields(x).Value + "</span></td>"""" + vbcrlf)")
```

Textarea

```
txtstream.WriteLine("Response.Write("""<td style=""""font-family:Calibri, Sans-
Serif;font-size: 12px;color:navy;""""  align='left'  nowrap='true'><textarea>"  +
rs.Fields(x).Value + "</textarea></td>"""" + vbcrlf)")
```

Textbox

```
        txtstream.WriteLine("Response.Write(""<td     style=""font-family:Calibri,
Sans-Serif;font-size:    12px;color:navy;""    align='left'    nowrap='true'><input
type=text value=""" + rs.Fields(x).Value + """></input></td>"" + vbcrlf)")
        rs.MoveNext
        loop
        txtstream.WriteLine("Response.Write(""</tr>"" + vbcrlf)")
    next
    txtstream.WriteLine("%>")
    txtstream.WriteLine("</table>")
    txtstream.WriteLine("</body>")
    txtstream.WriteLine("</html>")
    txtstream.Close()
```

HTA CODE

L IKE ASP AND ASPX, HTA BEEN AROUND FOR SOME TIME NOW. Despite the fact the concept appears to be old or outdated You should know that it is still being used as HTML as an EXE.

```
Set ws =  CreateObject("WScript.Shell")
Set fso =  CreateObject("Scripting.FileSystemObject")
Set txtstream =fso.OpenTextFile(ws.CurrentDirectory + "\Products.hta", 2, true,
-2)
txtstream.WriteLine("<html>")
txtstream.WriteLine("<head>")
txtstream.WriteLine("<HTA:APPLICATION ")
txtstream.WriteLine("ID = ""Products"" ")
txtstream.WriteLine("APPLICATIONNAME = ""Products"" ")
txtstream.WriteLine("SCROLL = ""yes"" ")
txtstream.WriteLine("SINGLEINSTANCE = ""yes"" ")
txtstream.WriteLine("WINDOWSTATE = ""maximize"" >")
txtstream.WriteLine("<title>" + Tablename + "</title>")
#Add Stylesheet here
txtstream.WriteLine("<body>")
txtstream.WriteLine("</br>")
```

Horizontal Reports

```
txtstream.WriteLine("<table border=0 cellspacing=3 cellpadding=3>")
txtstream.WriteLine("<tr>")
```

```vb
For x = 0 to rs.Fields.Count-1
    txtstream.WriteLine("<th style="" font-family:Calibri, Sans-Serif;font-size:
12px;color:darkred;"" align='left' nowrap='nowrap'>" + rs.Fields(x).Name +
"</th>")
Next
txtstream.WriteLine("</tr>")
Do While(rs.EOF = false)
    txtstream.WriteLine("<tr>")
    For x = 0 to rs.Fields.Count-1
```

NONE

```vb
        txtstream.WriteLine("<td style=""font-family:Calibri, Sans-Serif;font-
size: 12px;color:navy;"" align='left' nowrap='nowrap'>" + rs.Fields(x).Value +
"</td>")
```

Button

```vb
        txtstream.WriteLine("<td style=""font-family:Calibri, Sans-Serif;font-
size: 12px;color:navy;"" align='left' nowrap='true'><button style='width:100%;'
value ='" + rs.Fields(x).Value + "'>" + rs.Fields(x).Value + "</button></td>")
```

COMBOBOX

```vb
        txtstream.WriteLine("<td style=""font-family:Calibri, Sans-Serif;font-
size: 12px;color:navy;"" align='left' nowrap='true'><select><option value = """ +
rs.Fields(x).Value + """>" + rs.Fields(x).Value + "</option></select></td>")
```

DIV

```vb
        txtstream.WriteLine("<td style=""font-family:Calibri, Sans-Serif;font-
size: 12px;color:navy;"" align='left' nowrap='true'><div>" + rs.Fields(x).Value +
"</div></td>")
```

LINK

```
        txtstream.WriteLine("<td   style=""font-family:Calibri,   Sans-Serif;font-
size: 12px;color:navy;"" align='left' nowrap='true'><a href='" + rs.Fields(x).Value +
"'>" + rs.Fields(x).Value + "</a></td>")
```

LISTBOX

```
        txtstream.WriteLine("<td   style=""font-family:Calibri,   Sans-Serif;font-
size: 12px;color:navy;"" align='left' nowrap='true'><select multiple><option value =
"""" + rs.Fields(x).Value + """">" + rs.Fields(x).Value + "</option></select></td>")
```

SPAN

```
        txtstream.WriteLine("<td   style=""font-family:Calibri,   Sans-Serif;font-
size: 12px;color:navy;"" align='left' nowrap='true'><span>" + rs.Fields(x).Value +
"</span></td>")
```

TEXTAREA

```
        txtstream.WriteLine("<td   style=""font-family:Calibri,   Sans-Serif;font-
size: 12px;color:navy;"" align='left' nowrap='true'><textarea>" + rs.Fields(x).Value
+ "</textarea></td>")
```

TEXTBOX

```
        txtstream.WriteLine("<td   style=""font-family:Calibri,   Sans-Serif;font-
size: 12px;color:navy;"" align='left' nowrap='true'><input type=text value="""" +
rs.Fields(x).Value + """"></input></td>")
        Next
        txtstream.WriteLine("</tr>")
        rs.MoveNext
    Loop
    txtstream.WriteLine("</table>")
    txtstream.WriteLine("</body>")
    txtstream.WriteLine("</html>")
    txtstream.Close()
```

```
txtstream.WriteLine("<table border=0 cellspacing=3 cellpadding=3>")
For x = 0 to rs.Fields.Count-1
        txtstream.WriteLine("<tr><th    style=""    font-family:Calibri,    Sans-
Serif;font-size:    12px;color:darkred;""    align='left'    nowrap='nowrap'>"    +
rs.Fields(x).Name + "</th>")
        rs.MoveFirst()
        Do While(rs.EOF = false)
        txtstream.WriteLine("<td    style=""font-family:Calibri,    Sans-Serif;font-
size: 12px;color:navy;"">" + rs.Fields(x).Value + "</td>")
```

NONE

```
        txtstream.WriteLine("<td   style=""font-family:Calibri,   Sans-Serif;font-
size:  12px;color:navy;""  align='left'  nowrap='nowrap'>"  +  rs.Fields(x).Value  +
"</td>")
```

Button

```
        txtstream.WriteLine("<td    style=""font-family:Calibri,    Sans-Serif;font-
size:  12px;color:navy;""  align='left'  nowrap='true'><button  style='width:100%;'
value ='" + rs.Fields(x).Value + "'>" + rs.Fields(x).Value + "</button></td>")
```

Combobox

```
        txtstream.WriteLine("<td    style=""font-family:Calibri,    Sans-Serif;font-
size: 12px;color:navy;""  align='left'  nowrap='true'><select><option value = """"  +
rs.Fields(x).Value + """">" + rs.Fields(x).Value + "</option></select></td>")
```

Div

```
        txtstream.WriteLine("<td  style=""font-family:Calibri,  Sans-Serif;font-size:
12px;color:navy;""   align='left'   nowrap='true'><div>"   +   rs.Fields(x).Value   +
"</div></td>")
```

Link

```
txtstream.WriteLine("<td    style=""font-family:Calibri,    Sans-Serif;font-size:
12px;color:navy;""" align='left' nowrap='true'><a href='" + rs.Fields(x).Value + "'>"
+ rs.Fields(x).Value + "</a></td>")
```

Listbox

```
txtstream.WriteLine("<td    style=""font-family:Calibri,    Sans-Serif;font-size:
12px;color:navy;""" align='left' nowrap='true'><select multiple><option value = """"
+ rs.Fields(x).Value + """">" + rs.Fields(x).Value + "</option></select></td>")
```

Span

```
txtstream.WriteLine("<td style=""font-family:Calibri, Sans-Serif;font-size:
12px;color:navy;""" align='left' nowrap='true'><span>" + rs.Fields(x).Value +
"</span></td>")
```

Textarea

```
txtstream.WriteLine("<td    style=""font-family:Calibri,    Sans-Serif;font-size:
12px;color:navy;""" align='left' nowrap='true'><textarea>" + rs.Fields(x).Value +
"</textarea></td>")
```

Textbox

```
txtstream.WriteLine("<td    style=""font-family:Calibri,    Sans-Serif;font-
size: 12px;color:navy;""" align='left' nowrap='true'><input type=text value="""" +
rs.Fields(x).Value + """"></input></td>")
        rs.MoveNext
    Loop
    txtstream.WriteLine("</tr>")
Next
txtstream.WriteLine("</table>")
txtstream.WriteLine("</body>")
txtstream.WriteLine("</html>")
txtstream.Close()
```

```
txtstream.WriteLine("<table        style='border:Double;border-width:1px;border-
color:navy;' rules=all frames=both cellpadding=2 cellspacing=2 Width=0>")
txtstream.WriteLine("<tr>")
For x = 0 to rs.Fields.Count-1
    txtstream.WriteLine("<th style='"" font-family:Calibri, Sans-Serif;font-size:
12px;color:darkred;""  align='left'  nowrap='nowrap'>"  +  rs.Fields(x).Name  +
"</th>")
Next
txtstream.WriteLine("</tr>")
Do While(rs.EOF = false)
  txtstream.WriteLine("<tr>")
    For x = 0 to rs.Fields.Count-1
```

NONE

```
        txtstream.WriteLine("<td  style='""font-family:Calibri,  Sans-Serif;font-
size: 12px;color:navy;""  align='left'  nowrap='nowrap'>"  +  rs.Fields(x).Value  +
"</td>")
```

Button

```
        txtstream.WriteLine("<td  style='""font-family:Calibri,  Sans-Serif;font-
size: 12px;color:navy;""  align='left'  nowrap='true'><button  style='width:100%;'
value ='" + rs.Fields(x).Value + "'>" + rs.Fields(x).Value + "</button></td>")
```

COMBOBOX

```
        txtstream.WriteLine("<td  style='""font-family:Calibri,  Sans-Serif;font-
size: 12px;color:navy;""  align='left'  nowrap='true'><select><option value = """"  +
rs.Fields(x).Value + """">" + rs.Fields(x).Value + "</option></select></td>")
```

DIV

```
        txtstream.WriteLine("<td    style=""font-family:Calibri,    Sans-Serif;font-
size: 12px;color:navy;"" align='left' nowrap='true'><div>" + rs.Fields(x).Value +
"</div></td>")
```

LINK

```
        txtstream.WriteLine("<td    style=""font-family:Calibri,    Sans-Serif;font-
size: 12px;color:navy;"" align='left' nowrap='true'><a href='" + rs.Fields(x).Value +
"'>" + rs.Fields(x).Value + "</a></td>")
```

LISTBOX

```
        txtstream.WriteLine("<td    style=""font-family:Calibri,    Sans-Serif;font-
size: 12px;color:navy;"" align='left' nowrap='true'><select multiple><option value =
"""" + rs.Fields(x).Value + """">" + rs.Fields(x).Value + "</option></select></td>")
```

SPAN

```
        txtstream.WriteLine("<td    style=""font-family:Calibri,    Sans-Serif;font-
size: 12px;color:navy;"" align='left' nowrap='true'><span>" + rs.Fields(x).Value +
"</span></td>")
```

TEXTAREA

```
        txtstream.WriteLine("<td    style=""font-family:Calibri,    Sans-Serif;font-
size: 12px;color:navy;"" align='left' nowrap='true'><textarea>" + rs.Fields(x).Value
+ "</textarea></td>")
```

TEXTBOX

```
        txtstream.WriteLine("<td    style=""font-family:Calibri,    Sans-Serif;font-
size: 12px;color:navy;"" align='left' nowrap='true'><input type=text value="""" +
rs.Fields(x).Value + """"></input></td>")
    Next
    txtstream.WriteLine("</tr>")
    rs.MoveNext
Loop
txtstream.WriteLine("</table>")
txtstream.WriteLine("</body>")
```

```
txtstream.WriteLine("</html>")
txtstream.Close()
```

Vertical Tables

```
txtstream.WriteLine("<table        style='border:Double;border-width:1px;border-
color:navy;' rules=all frames=both cellpadding=2 cellspacing=2 Width=0>")
For x = 0 to rs.Fields.Count-1
        txtstream.WriteLine("<tr><th     style=""    font-family:Calibri,    Sans-
Serif;font-size:   12px;color:darkred;"""    align='left'    nowrap='nowrap'>"   +
rs.Fields(x).Name + "</th>")
        rs.MoveFirst()
        Do While rs.EOF = false
        txtstream.WriteLine("<td   style=""font-family:Calibri,   Sans-Serif;font-
size: 12px;color:navy;"">" + rs.Fields(x).Value + "</td>")
```

NONE

```
        txtstream.WriteLine("<td  style=""font-family:Calibri,  Sans-Serif;font-
size: 12px;color:navy;"" align='left' nowrap='nowrap'>" + rs.Fields(x).Value +
"</td>")
```

Button

```
        txtstream.WriteLine("<td   style=""font-family:Calibri,   Sans-Serif;font-
size: 12px;color:navy;"" align='left' nowrap='true'><button style='width:100%;'
value ='" + rs.Fields(x).Value + "'>" + rs.Fields(x).Value + "</button></td>")
```

Combobox

```
        txtstream.WriteLine("<td    style=""font-family:Calibri,   Sans-Serif;font-
size: 12px;color:navy;"" align='left' nowrap='true'><select><option value = """ +
rs.Fields(x).Value + """>" + rs.Fields(x).Value + "</option></select></td>")
```

Div

```
txtstream.WriteLine("<td style=""font-family:Calibri, Sans-Serif;font-size:
12px;color:navy;"" align='left' nowrap='true'><div>" + rs.Fields(x).Value +
"</div></td>")
```

Link

```
txtstream.WriteLine("<td style=""font-family:Calibri, Sans-Serif;font-size:
12px;color:navy;"" align='left' nowrap='true'><a href='" + rs.Fields(x).Value + "'>"
+ rs.Fields(x).Value + "</a></td>")
```

Listbox

```
txtstream.WriteLine("<td style=""font-family:Calibri, Sans-Serif;font-size:
12px;color:navy;"" align='left' nowrap='true'><select multiple><option value = """
+ rs.Fields(x).Value + """>" + rs.Fields(x).Value + "</option></select></td>")
```

Span

```
txtstream.WriteLine("<td style=""font-family:Calibri, Sans-Serif;font-size:
12px;color:navy;"" align='left' nowrap='true'><span>" + rs.Fields(x).Value +
"</span></td>")
```

Textarea

```
txtstream.WriteLine("<td style=""font-family:Calibri, Sans-Serif;font-size:
12px;color:navy;"" align='left' nowrap='true'><textarea>" + rs.Fields(x).Value +
"</textarea></td>")
```

Textbox

```
txtstream.WriteLine("<td style=""font-family:Calibri, Sans-Serif;font-
size: 12px;color:navy;"" align='left' nowrap='true'><input type=text value="""" +
rs.Fields(x).Value + """></input></td>")
        rs.MoveNext
    Loop
    txtstream.WriteLine("</tr>")
Next
txtstream.WriteLine("</table>")
```

```
txtstream.WriteLine("</body>")
txtstream.WriteLine("</html>")
txtstream.Close()
```

HTML CODE

WHAT CAN I SAY ABOUT HTML5 AND CSS THAT HASN'T BEEN SAID ALREADY? Well, I can say that it has come a long way since the 1990s.

```
Set ws = CreateObject("WScript.Shell")
Set fso = CreateObject("Scripting.FileSystemObject")
Set txtstream =fso.OpenTextFile(ws.CurrentDirectory + "\Products.html", 2,
true, -2)
txtstream.WriteLine("<html>")
txtstream.WriteLine("<head>")
txtstream.WriteLine("<title>" + Tablename + "</title>")
#Add Stylesheet here
txtstream.WriteLine("<body>")
txtstream.WriteLine("</br>")
```

Horizontal Reports

```
txtstream.WriteLine("<table border=0 cellspacing=3 cellpadding=3>")
txtstream.WriteLine("<tr>")
For x = 0 to rs.Fields.Count-1
```

txtstream.WriteLine("<th style="" font-family:Calibri, Sans-Serif;font-size: 12px;color:darkred;"" align='left' nowrap='nowrap'>" + rs.Fields(x).Name + "</th>")

txtstream.WriteLine("</tr>")
Next
Do While(rs.EOF = false)
  txtstream.WriteLine("<tr>")
  For x = 0 to rs.Fields.Count-1

NONE

txtstream.WriteLine("<td style=""font-family:Calibri, Sans-Serif;font-size: 12px;color:navy;"" align='left' nowrap='nowrap'>" + rs.Fields(x).Value + "</td>")

Button

txtstream.WriteLine("<td style=""font-family:Calibri, Sans-Serif;font-size: 12px;color:navy;"" align='left' nowrap='true'><button style='width:100%;' value ='" + rs.Fields(x).Value + "'>" + rs.Fields(x).Value + "</button></td>")

COMBOBOX

txtstream.WriteLine("<td style=""font-family:Calibri, Sans-Serif;font-size: 12px;color:navy;"" align='left' nowrap='true'><select><option value = """" + rs.Fields(x).Value + """">" + rs.Fields(x).Value + "</option></select></td>")

DIV

txtstream.WriteLine("<td style=""font-family:Calibri, Sans-Serif;font-size: 12px;color:navy;"" align='left' nowrap='true'> " + rs.Fields(x).Value + " </td>")

LINK

```vbscript
            txtstream.WriteLine("<td   style=""font-family:Calibri,  Sans-Serif;font-
size: 12px;color:navy;"" align='left' nowrap='true'><a href='" + rs.Fields(x).Value +
"'>" + rs.Fields(x).Value + "</a></td>")
```

LISTBOX

```vbscript
            txtstream.WriteLine("<td   style=""font-family:Calibri,  Sans-Serif;font-
size: 12px;color:navy;"" align='left' nowrap='true'><select multiple><option value =
"""" + rs.Fields(x).Value + """">" + rs.Fields(x).Value + "</option></select></td>")
```

SPAN

```vbscript
            txtstream.WriteLine("<td   style=""font-family:Calibri,  Sans-Serif;font-
size: 12px;color:navy;"" align='left' nowrap='true'><span>" + rs.Fields(x).Value +
"</span></td>")
```

TEXTAREA

```vbscript
            txtstream.WriteLine("<td   style=""font-family:Calibri,  Sans-Serif;font-
size: 12px;color:navy;"" align='left' nowrap='true'><textarea>" + rs.Fields(x).Value
+ "</textarea></td>")
```

TEXTBOX

```vbscript
            txtstream.WriteLine("<td   style=""font-family:Calibri,  Sans-Serif;font-
size: 12px;color:navy;"" align='left' nowrap='true'><input type=text value="""" +
rs.Fields(x).Value + """"></input></td>")
        Next
        txtstream.WriteLine("</tr>")
        rs.MoveNext
    Loop
    txtstream.WriteLine("</table>")
    txtstream.WriteLine("</body>")
    txtstream.WriteLine("</html>")
    txtstream.Close()
```

```
txtstream.WriteLine("<table border=0 cellspacing=3 cellpadding=3>")
For x = 0 to rs.Fields.Count-1
        txtstream.WriteLine("<tr><th    style=""    font-family:Calibri,    Sans-
Serif;font-size:    12px;color:darkred;"""    align='left'    nowrap='nowrap'>"    +
rs.Fields(x).Name + "</th>")
        rs.MoveFirst()
        Do While(rs.EOF = false)
        txtstream.WriteLine("<td    style=""font-family:Calibri,    Sans-Serif;font-
size: 12px;color:navy;"">" + rs.Fields(x).Value + "</td>")
```

NONE

```
        txtstream.WriteLine("<td  style=""font-family:Calibri,  Sans-Serif;font-
size:  12px;color:navy;"""  align='left'  nowrap='nowrap'>"  +  rs.Fields(x).Value  +
"</td>")
```

Button

```
        txtstream.WriteLine("<td    style=""font-family:Calibri,    Sans-Serif;font-
size:  12px;color:navy;"""  align='left'  nowrap='true'><button  style='width:100%;'
value ='" + rs.Fields(x).Value + "'>" + rs.Fields(x).Value + "</button></td>")
```

Combobox

```
        txtstream.WriteLine("<td    style=""font-family:Calibri,    Sans-Serif;font-
size: 12px;color:navy;"""  align='left'  nowrap='true'><select><option value = """" +
rs.Fields(x).Value + """">" + rs.Fields(x).Value + "</option></select></td>")
```

Div

```
        txtstream.WriteLine("<td  style=""font-family:Calibri,  Sans-Serif;font-size:
12px;color:navy;"""    align='left'    nowrap='true'><div>"    +    rs.Fields(x).Value    +
"</div></td>")
```

Link

```vb
txtstream.WriteLine("<td   style=""font-family:Calibri,   Sans-Serif;font-size:
12px;color:navy;"" align='left' nowrap='true'><a href='" + rs.Fields(x).Value + "'>"
+ rs.Fields(x).Value + "</a></td>")
```

Listbox

```vb
txtstream.WriteLine("<td   style=""font-family:Calibri,   Sans-Serif;font-size:
12px;color:navy;"" align='left' nowrap='true'><select multiple><option value = """"
+ rs.Fields(x).Value + """">" + rs.Fields(x).Value + "</option></select></td>")
```

Span

```vb
txtstream.WriteLine("<td style=""font-family:Calibri, Sans-Serif;font-size:
12px;color:navy;""  align='left'  nowrap='true'><span>" + rs.Fields(x).Value +
"</span></td>")
```

Textarea

```vb
txtstream.WriteLine("<td   style=""font-family:Calibri,   Sans-Serif;font-size:
12px;color:navy;""  align='left'  nowrap='true'><textarea>"  + rs.Fields(x).Value +
"</textarea></td>")
```

Textbox

```vb
txtstream.WriteLine("<td   style=""font-family:Calibri,   Sans-Serif;font-
size: 12px;color:navy;"" align='left' nowrap='true'><input type=text value="""" +
rs.Fields(x).Value + """"></input></td>")
        rs.MoveNext
    Loop
    txtstream.WriteLine("</tr>")
Next
txtstream.WriteLine("</table>")
txtstream.WriteLine("</body>")
txtstream.WriteLine("</html>")
txtstream.Close()
```

```
txtstream.WriteLine("<table        style='border:Double;border-width:1px;border-
color:navy;' rules=all frames=both cellpadding=2 cellspacing=2 Width=0>")
txtstream.WriteLine("<tr>")
For x = 0 to rs.Fields.Count-1
   txtstream.WriteLine("<th style="" font-family:Calibri, Sans-Serif;font-size:
12px;color:darkred;"" align='left' nowrap='nowrap'>" + rs.Fields(x).Name +
"</th>")
Next
txtstream.WriteLine("</tr>")
Do While(rs.EOF = false)
   txtstream.WriteLine("<tr>")
      For x = 0 to rs.Fields.Count-1
```

NONE

```
      txtstream.WriteLine("<td   style=""font-family:Calibri,   Sans-Serif;font-
size: 12px;color:navy;""  align='left'  nowrap='nowrap'>" + rs.Fields(x).Value +
"</td>")
```

Button

```
      txtstream.WriteLine("<td   style=""font-family:Calibri,   Sans-Serif;font-
size: 12px;color:navy;""  align='left'  nowrap='true'><button style='width:100%;'
value ='" + rs.Fields(x).Value + "'>" + rs.Fields(x).Value + "</button></td>")
```

COMBOBOX

```
      txtstream.WriteLine("<td   style=""font-family:Calibri,   Sans-Serif;font-
size: 12px;color:navy;""  align='left'  nowrap='true'><select><option value = """ +
rs.Fields(x).Value + """>" + rs.Fields(x).Value + "</option></select></td>")
```

DIV

```
      txtstream.WriteLine("<td   style=""font-family:Calibri,   Sans-Serif;font-
size: 12px;color:navy;""  align='left'  nowrap='true'><div>" + rs.Fields(x).Value +
"</div></td>")
```

LINK

```
txtstream.WriteLine("<td style=""font-family:Calibri, Sans-Serif;font-size: 12px;color:navy;"" align='left' nowrap='true'><a href='" + rs.Fields(x).Value + "'>" + rs.Fields(x).Value + "</a></td>")
```

LISTBOX

```
txtstream.WriteLine("<td style=""font-family:Calibri, Sans-Serif;font-size: 12px;color:navy;"" align='left' nowrap='true'><select multiple><option value = """" + rs.Fields(x).Value + """">" + rs.Fields(x).Value + "</option></select></td>")
```

SPAN

```
txtstream.WriteLine("<td style=""font-family:Calibri, Sans-Serif;font-size: 12px;color:navy;"" align='left' nowrap='true'><span>" + rs.Fields(x).Value + "</span></td>")
```

TEXTAREA

```
txtstream.WriteLine("<td style=""font-family:Calibri, Sans-Serif;font-size: 12px;color:navy;"" align='left' nowrap='true'><textarea>" + rs.Fields(x).Value + "</textarea></td>")
```

TEXTBOX

```
txtstream.WriteLine("<td style=""font-family:Calibri, Sans-Serif;font-size: 12px;color:navy;"" align='left' nowrap='true'><input type=text value="""" + rs.Fields(x).Value + """"></input></td>")
        Next
        txtstream.WriteLine("</tr>")
        rs.MoveNext
    Loop
    txtstream.WriteLine("</table>")
    txtstream.WriteLine("</body>")
    txtstream.WriteLine("</html>")
    txtstream.Close()
```

Vertical Tables

txtstream.WriteLine("<table   style='border:Double;border-width:1px;border-color:navy;' rules=all frames=both cellpadding=2 cellspacing=2 Width=0>")

For x = 0 to rs.Fields.Count-1

txtstream.WriteLine("<tr><th   style=""   font-family:Calibri,   Sans-Serif;font-size: 12px;color:darkred;""   align='left'   nowrap='nowrap'>"   +   rs.Fields(x).Name + "</th>")

rs.MoveFirst()

Do While rs.EOF = false

txtstream.WriteLine("<td   style=""font-family:Calibri,   Sans-Serif;font-size: 12px;color:navy;"">" + rs.Fields(x).Value + "</td>")

NONE

txtstream.WriteLine("<td   style=""font-family:Calibri,   Sans-Serif;font-size: 12px;color:navy;""   align='left'   nowrap='nowrap'>" + rs.Fields(x).Value + "</td>")

Button

txtstream.WriteLine("<td   style=""font-family:Calibri,   Sans-Serif;font-size: 12px;color:navy;""   align='left'   nowrap='true'><button style='width:100%;' value ='" + rs.Fields(x).Value + "'>" + rs.Fields(x).Value + "</button></td>")

Combobox

txtstream.WriteLine("<td   style=""font-family:Calibri,   Sans-Serif;font-size: 12px;color:navy;""   align='left'   nowrap='true'><select><option value = """ + rs.Fields(x).Value + """>" + rs.Fields(x).Value + "</option></select></td>")

Div

txtstream.WriteLine("<td   style=""font-family:Calibri,   Sans-Serif;font-size: 12px;color:navy;""   align='left'   nowrap='true'> "   +   rs.Fields(x).Value   + " </td>")

Link

```
txtstream.WriteLine("<td style=""font-family:Calibri, Sans-Serif;font-size:
12px;color:navy;"" align='left' nowrap='true'><a href='" + rs.Fields(x).Value + "'>"
+ rs.Fields(x).Value + "</a></td>")
```

Listbox

```
txtstream.WriteLine("<td style=""font-family:Calibri, Sans-Serif;font-size:
12px;color:navy;"" align='left' nowrap='true'><select multiple><option value = """"
+ rs.Fields(x).Value + """">" + rs.Fields(x).Value + "</option></select></td>")
```

Span

```
txtstream.WriteLine("<td style=""font-family:Calibri, Sans-Serif;font-size:
12px;color:navy;"" align='left' nowrap='true'><span>" + rs.Fields(x).Value +
"</span></td>")
```

Textarea

```
txtstream.WriteLine("<td style=""font-family:Calibri, Sans-Serif;font-size:
12px;color:navy;"" align='left' nowrap='true'><textarea>" + rs.Fields(x).Value +
"</textarea></td>")
```

Textbox

```
txtstream.WriteLine("<td style=""font-family:Calibri, Sans-Serif;font-
size: 12px;color:navy;"" align='left' nowrap='true'><input type=text value="""" +
rs.Fields(x).Value + """"></input></td>")
        rs.MoveNext
    Loop
    txtstream.WriteLine("</tr>")
Next
txtstream.WriteLine("</table>")
txtstream.WriteLine("</body>")
txtstream.WriteLine("</html>")
txtstream.Close()
```

DELIMITED FILES

THERE ARE MANY DIFFERENT KINDS OF DELIMITED FILES. The ones we are going to be using are the most common ones. And by Common, this will include:

- Colon Delimited
- Comma Delimited
- Exclamation Delimited
- Semi-Colon Delimited
- Tab Delimited
- Tilde Delimited

Essentially, the only differences in the code is how the delimiter is used, but the code examples are also going to show you how the information can be arranged in both Horizontal and Vertical Views.

```
Set ws = CreateObject("WScript.Shell")
Set fso = CreateObject("Scripting.FileSystemObject")
Set txtstream =fso.OpenTextFile(ws.CurrentDirectory + "\Products.txt", 2,
true, -2)
tstr= ""
For x = 0 to rs.Fields.Count-1
   if tstr <> "" Then
      tstr = tstr + ":"
   End If
   tstr = tstr + rs.Fields(x).Name
Next
txtstream.Writeline(tstr)
tstr = ""
rs.MoveFirst()
Do While(rs.EOF = false)
   For x = 0 to rs.Fields.Count-1
      if tstr <> "" Then
         tstr = tstr + ":"
      End If
      tstr = tstr + chr(34) + rs.Fields(x).Value + chr(34)
   Next
   txtstream.Writeline(tstr)
   tstr = ""
   rs.MoveNext
Loop
```

```
For x = 0 to rs.Fields.Count-1
   tstr = rs.Fields(x).Name
   rs.MoveFirst()
   Do While(rs.EOF = false)
      if tstr <> "" Then
         tstr = tstr + ":"
      End If
```

```
            tstr = tstr + chr(34) + rs.Fields(x).Value + chr(34)
            rs.MoveNext
        Loop
        txtstream.Writeline(tstr)
        tstr = ""
    Next
    txtstream.Close
```

COMMA DELIMITED HORIZONTAL

```
    Set ws =  CreateObject("WScript.Shell")
    Set fso =  CreateObject("Scripting.FileSystemObject")
    Set  txtstream =fso.OpenTextFile(ws.CurrentDirectory  +  "\Products.csv",  2,
true, -2)
    tstr= ""
    For x = 0 to rs.Fields.Count-1
        if tstr <> "" Then
            tstr = tstr + ","
        End If
        tstr = tstr + rs.Fields(x).Name
    Next
    txtstream.Writeline(tstr)
    tstr = ""
    rs.MoveFirst()
    Do While(rs.EOF = false)
        For x = 0 to rs.Fields.Count-1
            if tstr <> "" Then
                tstr = tstr + ","
            End If
            tstr = tstr + chr(34) + rs.Fields(x).Value + chr(34)
        Next
        txtstream.Writeline(tstr)
        tstr = ""
        rs.MoveNext
    Loop
```

COMMA DELIMITED VERTICAL

```
Set ws = CreateObject("WScript.Shell")
Set fso = CreateObject("Scripting.FileSystemObject")
Set txtstream =fso.OpenTextFile(ws.CurrentDirectory + "\Products.csv", 2,
true, -2)

For x = 0 to rs.Fields.Count-1
  tstr = rs.Fields(x).Name
  rs.MoveFirst()
  Do While(rs.EOF = false)
    if tstr <> "" Then
      tstr = tstr + ","
    End If
    tstr = tstr + chr(34) + rs.Fields(x).Value + chr(34)
    rs.MoveNext
  Loop
  txtstream.Writeline(tstr)
  tstr = ""
Next
txtstream.Close
```

EXCLAMATION DELIMITED HORIZONTAL

```
Set ws = CreateObject("WScript.Shell")
Set fso = CreateObject("Scripting.FileSystemObject")
Set txtstream =fso.OpenTextFile(ws.CurrentDirectory + "\Products.txt", 2,
true, -2)
tstr= ""
For x = 0 to rs.Fields.Count-1
  if tstr <> "" Then
    tstr = tstr + "!"
  End If
  tstr = tstr + rs.Fields(x).Name
Next
txtstream.Writeline(tstr)
```

```
      tstr = ""
      rs.MoveFirst()
      Do While(rs.EOF = false)
         For x = 0 to rs.Fields.Count-1
            if tstr <> "" Then
               tstr = tstr + "!"
            End If
            tstr = tstr + chr(34) + rs.Fields(x).Value + chr(34)
         Next
         txtstream.Writeline(tstr)
         tstr = ""
         rs.MoveNext
      Loop
```

EXCLAMATION DELIMITED VERTICAL

```
      Set ws = CreateObject("WScript.Shell")
      Set fso = CreateObject("Scripting.FileSystemObject")
      Set txtstream =fso.OpenTextFile(ws.CurrentDirectory + "\Products.txt", 2,
true, -2)

      For x = 0 to rs.Fields.Count-1
         tstr = rs.Fields(x).Name
         rs.MoveFirst()
         Do While(rs.EOF = false)
            if tstr <> "" Then
               tstr = tstr + "!"
            End If
            tstr = tstr + chr(34) + rs.Fields(x).Value + chr(34)
            rs.MoveNext
         Loop
         txtstream.Writeline(tstr)
         tstr = ""
      Next
      txtstream.Close
```

```
Set ws = CreateObject("WScript.Shell")
Set fso = CreateObject("Scripting.FileSystemObject")
Set txtstream =fso.OpenTextFile(ws.CurrentDirectory + "\Products.txt", 2,
true, -2)
tstr= ""
For x = 0 to rs.Fields.Count-1
  if tstr <> "" Then
    tstr = tstr + ";"
  End If
  tstr = tstr + rs.Fields(x).Name
Next
txtstream.Writeline(tstr)
tstr = ""
rs.MoveFirst()
Do While(rs.EOF = false)
  For x = 0 to rs.Fields.Count-1
    if tstr <> "" Then
      tstr = tstr + ";"
    End If
    tstr = tstr + chr(34) + rs.Fields(x).Value + chr(34)
  Next
  txtstream.Writeline(tstr)
  tstr = ""
  rs.MoveNext
Loop
```

```
Set ws = CreateObject("WScript.Shell")
Set fso = CreateObject("Scripting.FileSystemObject")
Set txtstream =fso.OpenTextFile(ws.CurrentDirectory + "\Products.txt", 2,
true, -2)

For x = 0 to rs.Fields.Count-1
  tstr = rs.Fields(x).Name
  rs.MoveFirst()
```

```
      Do While(rs.EOF = false)
        if tstr <> "" Then
          tstr = tstr + ";"
        End If
        tstr = tstr + chr(34) + rs.Fields(x).Value + chr(34)
        rs.MoveNext
      Loop
      txtstream.Writeline(tstr)
      tstr = ""
    Next
    txtstream.Close
```

TAB DELIMITED HORIZONTAL

```
    Set ws = CreateObject("WScript.Shell")
    Set fso = CreateObject("Scripting.FileSystemObject")
    Set txtstream =fso.OpenTextFile(ws.CurrentDirectory + "\Products.txt", 2,
true, -2)
    tstr= ""

    For x = 0 to rs.Fields.Count-1
      if tstr <> "" Then
        tstr = tstr + vbTab
      End If
      tstr = tstr + rs.Fields(x).Name
    Next
    txtstream.Writeline(tstr)
    tstr = ""
    rs.MoveFirst()
    Do While(rs.EOF = false)
      For x = 0 to rs.Fields.Count-1
        if tstr <> "" Then
          tstr = tstr + vbTab
        End If
        tstr = tstr + chr(34) + rs.Fields(x).Value + chr(34)
      Next
      txtstream.Writeline(tstr)
      tstr = ""
```

```
        rs.MoveNext
    Loop
```

```
    Set ws =  CreateObject("WScript.Shell")
    Set fso =  CreateObject("Scripting.FileSystemObject")
    Set  txtstream  =fso.OpenTextFile(ws.CurrentDirectory  +  "\Products.txt",  2,
true, -2)

    For x = 0 to rs.Fields.Count-1
      tstr = rs.Fields(x).Name
      rs.MoveFirst()
      Do While(rs.EOF = false)
        if tstr <> "" Then
          tstr = tstr + vbTab
        End If
        tstr = tstr + chr(34) + rs.Fields(x).Value + chr(34)
        rs.MoveNext
      Loop
      txtstream.Writeline(tstr)
      tstr = ""
    Next
    txtstream.Close
```

```
    Set ws =  CreateObject("WScript.Shell")
    Set fso =  CreateObject("Scripting.FileSystemObject")
    Set  txtstream  =fso.OpenTextFile(ws.CurrentDirectory  +  "\Products.txt",  2,
true, -2)
    tstr= ""
    For x = 0 to rs.Fields.Count-1
      if tstr <> "" Then
        tstr = tstr + "~"
```

```
            End If
         tstr = tstr + rs.Fields(x).Name
      Next
      txtstream.Writeline(tstr)
      tstr = ""
      rs.MoveFirst()
      Do While(rs.EOF = false)
         For x = 0 to rs.Fields.Count-1
            if tstr <> "" Then
               tstr = tstr + "~"
            End If
            tstr = tstr + chr(34) + rs.Fields(x).Value + chr(34)
         Next
         txtstream.Writeline(tstr)
         tstr = ""
         rs.MoveNext
      Loop
```

TILDE DELIMITED VERTICAL

```
      Set ws = CreateObject("WScript.Shell")
      Set fso = CreateObject("Scripting.FileSystemObject")
      Set txtstream =fso.OpenTextFile(ws.CurrentDirectory + "\Products.txt", 2,
true, -2)
      For x = 0 to rs.Fields.Count-1
         tstr = rs.Fields(x).Name
         rs.MoveFirst()
         Do While(rs.EOF = false)
            if tstr <> "" Then
               tstr = tstr + "~"
            End If
            tstr = tstr + chr(34) + rs.Fields(x).Value + chr(34)
            rs.MoveNext
         Loop
         txtstream.Writeline(tstr)
         tstr = ""
      Next
      txtstream.Close
```

XML FILES

n this section of the book, we're going to be Coding for the creation of Attribute XML Element XML, Element XML for XSL and Schema XML

```
ws  = CreateObject("WScript.Shell")
fso  = CreateObject("Scripting.FileSystemObject")
txtstream  = fso.OpenTextFile("C:\Products.xml", 2, true, -2)
txtstream.WriteLine("<?xml version='1.0' encoding='iso-8859-1'?>")
txtstream.WriteLine("<data>")
rs.MoveFirst()
Do While(rs.EOF = false)
   txtstream.WriteLine("<Products>")
   For x in range(rs.Fields.Count):
     txtstream.WriteLine("<property name = """" + rs.Fields(x).Name + """"
value=""""" + rs.Fields(x).value + """""/>")
   Next
   txtstream.WriteLine("</Products>")
rs.MoveNext()
Loop
txtstream.WriteLine("</data>")
txtstream.Close
```

```
Set xmldoc = CreateObject("MSXML2.DOMDocument")
Set pi = xmldoc.CreateProcessingInstruction("xml",    "version='1.0'
encoding='ISO-8859-1'")
Set oRoot = xmldoc.CreateElement("data")
xmldoc.AppendChild(pi)
Do While rs.EOF = false
  Set oNode = xmldoc.CreateNode(1, "Products", "")
  for x in range(rs.Fields.Count):
    Set oNode1 = xmldoc.CreateNode(1, "Property", "")
    Set oAtt = xmldoc.CreateAttribute("NAME")
    oAtt.Value = rs.Fields(x).Name
    oNode1.Attributes.SetNamedItem(oAtt)
    Set oAtt = xmldoc.CreateAttribute("DATATYPE")
    oAtt.Value = str(rs.Fields(x).Type.Name))
    oNode1.Attributes.SetNamedItem(oAtt)
    Set oAtt = xmldoc.CreateAttribute("SIZE")
    oAtt.Value = str(rs.Fields(x).Value.)
    oNode1.Attributes.SetNamedItem(oAtt)
    Set oAtt = xmldoc.CreateAttribute("Value")
    oAtt.Value = GetValue(prop, obj)
    oNode1.Attributes.SetNamedItem(oAtt)
    oNode.AppendChild(oNode1)
  Next
  oRoot.AppendChild(oNode)
Loop
xmldoc.AppendChild(oRoot)
Set ws = CreateObject("WScript.Shell")
xmldoc.Save(ws.CurrentDirectory + "\\Products.xml")
```

```
Set ws = CreateObject("WScript.Shell")
Set fso = CreateObject("Scripting.FileSystemObject")
Set txtstream =fso.OpenTextFile(ws.CurrentDirectory + "\Products.txt", 2,
true, -2)
txtstream.WriteLine("<?xml version='1.0' encoding='iso-8859-1'?>")
txtstream.WriteLine("<data>")
rs.MoveFirst
Do While(rs.EOF = false)
    txtstream.WriteLine("<Products>")
    For x = 0 to rs.Fields.Count-1
        txtstream.WriteLine("<" + rs.Fields(x).Name + ">" + rs.Fields(x).Value +
"</" + rs.Fields(x).Name + ">")
    Next
    txtstream.WriteLine("</Products>")
    rs.MoveNext()
Loop
txtstream.WriteLine("</data>")
txtstream.close()
```

ELEMENT XML USING THE DOM

```
Set xmldoc = CreateObject("MSXML2.DOMDocument")
 Set pi = xmldoc.CreateProcessingInstruction("xml", "version='1.0'
encoding='ISO-8859-1'")

Set oRoot = xmldoc.CreateElement("data")
xmldoc.AppendChild(pi)
Do While rs.EOF = false
    Set oNode = xmldoc.CreateNode(1, "Products", "")
    for x = 0 to rs.Fields.Count -1
        Set oNode1 = xmldoc.CreateNode(1, rs.Fields(x),Name, "")
        oNode1.Text = str(rs.Fields(x).Value)
        Call oNode.AppendChild(oNode1)
    Next
    Call oRoot.AppendChild(oNode)
    rs.MoveNext
Loop
```

```
Call xmldoc.AppendChild(oRoot)
Set ws = CreateObject("WScript.Shell")
xmldoc.Save(ws.CurrentDirectory + "\\Products.xml")
```

ELEMENT XML FOR XSL USING A TEXT FILE

```
Set ws = CreateObject("WScript.Shell")
Set fso = CreateObject("Scripting.FileSystemObject")
Set txtstream =fso.OpenTextFile(ws.CurrentDirectory + "\Products.txt", 2,
true, -2)
    txtstream.WriteLine("<?xml version='1.0' encoding='iso-8859-1'?>")
    txtstream.WriteLine("<?xml-stylesheet        type='Text/xsl'      href='"      +
ws.CurrentDirectory + "\Products.xsl"?>
    txtstream.WriteLine("<?xml version='1.0' encoding='iso-8859-1'?>")
    txtstream.WriteLine("<data>")
    rs.MoveFirst
    Do While(rs.EOF = false)
       txtstream.WriteLine("<Products>")
       For x = 0 to rs.Fields.Count-1
          txtstream.WriteLine("<" + rs.Fields(x).Name + ">" + rs.Fields(x).Value +
"</" + rs.Fields(x).Name + ">")
       Next
       txtstream.WriteLine("</Products>")
       rs.MoveNext()
    Loop
    txtstream.WriteLine("</data>")
    txtstream.close()
```

ELEMENT XML FOR XSL USING THE DOM

```
Set xmldoc = CreateObject("MSXML2.DOMDocument")
Set   pi   =   xmldoc.CreateProcessingInstruction("xml",      "version='1.0'
    encoding='ISO-8859-1'")
Set pii = xmldoc.CreateProcessingInstruction("xml-stylesheet", "type='text/xsl'
href='Process.xsl'")
Set oRoot = xmldoc.CreateElement("data")
xmldoc.AppendChild(pi)
```

```
xmldoc.AppendChild(pii)
Do While rs.EOF = false
    Set oNode = xmldoc.CreateNode(1, "Products", "")
    for x = 0 to rs.Fields.Count -1
        Set oNode1 = xmldoc.CreateNode(1, rs.Fields(x),Name, "")
        oNode1.Text = str(rs.Fields(x).Value)
        Call oNode.AppendChild(oNode1)
    Next
    Call oRoot.AppendChild(oNode)
    rs.MoveNext
Loop
Call xmldoc.AppendChild(oRoot)
Set ws = CreateObject("WScript.Shell")
xmldoc.Save(ws.CurrentDirectory + "\\Products.xml")
```

SCHEMA XML USING A TEXT FILE

```
Set ws = CreateObject("WScript.Shell")
Set fso = CreateObject("Scripting.FileSystemObject")
Set txtstream =fso.OpenTextFile(ws.CurrentDirectory + "\Products.txt", 2,
true, -2)
txtstream.WriteLine("<?xml version='1.0' encoding='iso-8859-1'?>")
txtstream.WriteLine("<data>")
rs.MoveFirst
Do While(rs.EOF = false)
    txtstream.WriteLine("<Products>")
    For x = 0 to rs.Fields.Count-1
        txtstream.WriteLine("<" + rs.Fields(x).Name + ">" + rs.Fields(x).Value +
"</" + rs.Fields(x).Name + ">")
    Next
    txtstream.WriteLine("</Products>")
    rs.MoveNext()
Loop
txtstream.WriteLine("</data>")
txtstream.close()
rs1 = CreateObject("ADODB.Recordset")
```

```
    rs1.ActiveConnection          =          "Provider=MSDAOSP;          Data
Source=msxml2.DSOControl"
    rs1.Open(ws.CurrentDirectory + "\Products.xml")

    If (fso.FileExists(ws.CurrentDirectory + "\Products_Schema.xml") = true)
Then
        fso.DeleteFile(ws.CurrentDirectory + "\Products_Schema.xml")


    rs.Save(ws.CurrentDirectory + "\Products_Schema.xml", 1)
```

SCHEMA XML USING THE DOM

```
    Set xmldoc = CreateObject("MSXML2.DOMDocument")
    Set pi = xmldoc.CreateProcessingInstruction("xml", "version='1.0'
encoding='ISO-8859-1'")
    Set oRoot = xmldoc.CreateElement("data")
    xmldoc.AppendChild(pi)
    Do While rs.EOF = false
        Set oNode = xmldoc.CreateNode(1, "Products", "")
    for x = 0 to rs.Fields.Count -1
        Set oNode1 = xmldoc.CreateNode(1, rs.Fields(x),Name, "")
        oNode1.Text = str(rs.Fields(x).Value)
        Call oNode.AppendChild(oNode1)
    Next
    Call oRoot.AppendChild(oNode)
    rs.MoveNext
Loop
Call xmldoc.AppendChild(oRoot)
Set ws = CreateObject("WScript.Shell")
xmldoc.Save(ws.CurrentDirectory + "\\Products.xml")


    rs1 = CreateObject("ADODB.Recordset")
    rs1.ActiveConnection = "Provider=MSDAOSP; Data
Source=msxml2.DSOControl"
    rs1.Open(ws.CurrentDirectory + "\Products.xml")
```

```
    If  (fso.FileExists(ws.CurrentDirectory  +  "\Products_Schema.xml")  =  true)
Then
        fso.DeleteFile(ws.CurrentDirectory + "\Products_Schema.xml")


    rs.Save(ws.CurrentDirectory + "\Products_Schema.xml", 1)
```

EXCEL CODING EXAMPLES

BELOW ARE SOME EXAMPLES OF ADO DRIVING EXCEL VISUAL RENDERINGS.

EXCEL CODE IN HORIZONTAL FORMAT USING A CSV FILE

```
Set ws = CreateObject("WScript.Shell")
Set fso = CreateObject("Scripting.FileSystemObject")
Set txtstream =fso.OpenTextFile(ws.CurrentDirectory + "\Products.csv", 2,
true, -2)
tstr= ""


For x = 0 to rs.Fields.Count-1
   if tstr <> "" Then
      tstr = tstr + ","
   End If
   tstr = tstr + rs.Fields(x).Name
Next
txtstream.Writeline(tstr)
tstr = ""
```

```
    rs.MoveFirst()
    Do While(rs.EOF = false)
       For x = 0 to rs.Fields.Count-1
          if tstr <> "" Then
             tstr = tstr + ","
          End If
          tstr = tstr + chr(34) + rs.Fields(x).Value + chr(34)
       Next
       txtstream.Writeline(tstr)
       tstr = ""
       rs.MoveNext
    Loop
```

EXCEL CODE IN VERTICAL FORMAT USING A CSV FILE

```
    Set ws = CreateObject("WScript.Shell")
    Set fso = CreateObject("Scripting.FileSystemObject")
    Set txtstream =fso.OpenTextFile(ws.CurrentDirectory + "\Products.csv", 2,
true, -2)
    tstr= ""
    For x = 0 to rs.Fields.Count-1
       tstr = rs.Fields(x).Name
       rs.MoveFirst()
       Do While(rs.EOF = false)
          if tstr <> "" Then
             tstr = tstr + ","
          End If
          tstr = tstr + chr(34) + rs.Fields(x).Value + chr(34)
          rs.MoveNext
       Loop
       txtstream.Writeline(tstr)
       tstr = ""
    Next
    txtstream.Close

    ws.Run(ws.CurrentDirectory + "\Products.csv")
```

```
Set oExcel = CreateObject("Excel.Application")
oExcel.Visible = true
Set wb = oExcel.Workbooks.Add()
Set ws = wb.WorkSheets(1)
ws.Name = "Products"
y=2
For x = 0 to rs.Fields.Count-1
    ws.Cells.Item(1, x+1) = rs.Fields(x).Name
Next
rs.MoveFirst()
Do While rs.EOF = False
    For x = 0 to rs.Fields.Count-1
        ws.Cells.Item(y, x +1) = rs.Fields(x).Value
    Next
    y=y+1
    rs.MoveNext
Loop

ws.Columns.HorizontalAlignment = -4131
iret = ws.Columns.AutoFit()
```

```
oExcel = CreateObject("Excel.Application")
oExcel.Visible = true
wb = oExcel.Workbooks.Add()
Set ws = wb.WorkSheets(1)
ws.Name = "Products"
y=2
For x = 0 to rs.Fields.Count-1
    ws.Cells.Item(x+1, 1) = rs.Fields(x).Name
Next
rs.MoveFirst()
Do While rs.EOF = False
    For x = 0 to rs.Fields.Count-1
        ws.Cells.Item(x +1, y) = rs.Fields(x).Value
```

```
        Next
        y=y+1
        rs.MoveNext
    Loop

    ws.Columns.HorizontalAlignment = -4131
    iret = ws.Columns.AutoFit()
```

```
Set ws = CreateObject("WScript.Shell")
Set fso = CreateObject("Scripting.FileSystemObject")
Set txtstream =fso.OpenTextFile(ws.CurrentDirectory + "\\ProcessExcel.xml", 2,
true, -2)
txtstream.WriteLine("<?xml version='1.0'?>")
txtstream.WriteLine("<?mso-application progid='Excel.Sheet'?>")
txtstream.WriteLine("<Workbook            xmlns='urn:schemas-microsoft-
com:office:spreadsheet'     xmlns:o='urn:schemas-microsoft-com:office:office'
xmlns:x='urn:schemas-microsoft-com:office:excel'        xmlns:ss='urn:schemas-
microsoft-com:office:spreadsheet'        xmlns:html='http://www.w3.org/TR/REC-
html40'>")
txtstream.WriteLine(" <DocumentProperties    xmlns='urn:schemas-microsoft-
com:office:office'>")
txtstream.WriteLine("            <Author>Windows User</Author>")
txtstream.WriteLine("            <LastAuthor>Windows User</LastAuthor>")
txtstream.WriteLine("            <Created>2007-11-27T19:36:16Z</Created>")
txtstream.WriteLine("            <Version>12.00</Version>")
txtstream.WriteLine(" </DocumentProperties>")
txtstream.WriteLine(" <ExcelWorkbook          xmlns='urn:schemas-microsoft-
com:office:excel'>")
txtstream.WriteLine("            <WindowHeight>11835</WindowHeight>")
txtstream.WriteLine("            <WindowWidth>18960</WindowWidth>")
txtstream.WriteLine("            <WindowTopX>120</WindowTopX>")
txtstream.WriteLine("            <WindowTopY>135</WindowTopY>")
txtstream.WriteLine("            <ProtectStructure>False</ProtectStructure>")
txtstream.WriteLine("            <ProtectWindows>False</ProtectWindows>")
```

```
txtstream.WriteLine(" </ExcelWorkbook>")
txtstream.WriteLine(" <Styles>")
txtstream.WriteLine("                    <Style ss:ID='Default' ss:Name='Normal'>")
txtstream.WriteLine("                        <Alignment ss:Vertical='Bottom'/>")
txtstream.WriteLine("                        <Borders/>")
txtstream.WriteLine("                        <Font                ss:FontName='Calibri'
x:Family='Swiss' ss:Size='11' ss:Color='#000000'/>")
txtstream.WriteLine("                        <Interior/>")
txtstream.WriteLine("                        <NumberFormat/>")
txtstream.WriteLine("                        <Protection/>")
txtstream.WriteLine("                    </Style>")
txtstream.WriteLine("                    <Style ss:ID='s62'>")
txtstream.WriteLine("                        <Borders/>")
txtstream.WriteLine("                        <Font                ss:FontName='Calibri'
x:Family='Swiss' ss:Size='11' ss:Color='#000000' ss:Bold='1'/>")
txtstream.WriteLine("                    </Style>")
txtstream.WriteLine("                    <Style ss:ID='s63'>")
txtstream.WriteLine("                        <Alignment            ss:Horizontal='Left'
ss:Vertical='Bottom' ss:Indent='2'/>")
txtstream.WriteLine("                        <Font                ss:FontName='Verdana'
x:Family='Swiss' ss:Size='7.7' ss:Color='#000000'/>")
txtstream.WriteLine("                    </Style>")
txtstream.WriteLine(" </Styles>")
txtstream.WriteLine("<Worksheet ss:Name='Process'>")
txtstream.WriteLine("                    <Table    x:FullColumns='1'    x:FullRows='1'
ss:DefaultRowHeight='24.9375'>")
txtstream.WriteLine("                        <Column  ss:AutoFitWidth='1'  ss:Width='82.5'
ss:Span='5'/>")
txtstream.WriteLine("        <Row ss:AutoFitHeight='0'>")
For x = 0 To rs.Fields.Count-1
        txtstream.WriteLine("                        <Cell   ss:StyleID='s62'><Data
ss:Type='String'>" + rs.Fields(x).Name + "</Data></Cell>")
    Next
    txtstream.WriteLine("        </Row>")
    Do While rs.EOF = false
        txtstream.WriteLine("        <Row ss:AutoFitHeight='0' ss:Height='13.5'>")
        For x = 0 To rs.Fields.Count-1
        txtstream.WriteLine("                <Cell><Data ss:Type='String'><![CDATA(" +
str(rs.Fields(x).Value)) + "))></Data></Cell>")
    Next
```

```vbnet
        txtstream.WriteLine("    </Row>")
        rs.MoveNext()
    Loop
    txtstream.WriteLine("  </Table>")
    txtstream.WriteLine("  <WorksheetOptions          xmlns='urn:schemas-microsoft-com:office:excel'>")
    txtstream.WriteLine("   <PageSetup>")
    txtstream.WriteLine("    <Header x:Margin='0.3'/>")
    txtstream.WriteLine("    <Footer x:Margin='0.3'/>")
    txtstream.WriteLine("    <PageMargins          x:Bottom='0.75' x:Left='0.7' x:Right='0.7' x:Top='0.75'/>")
    txtstream.WriteLine("   </PageSetup>")
    txtstream.WriteLine("   <Unsynced/>")
    txtstream.WriteLine("   <Print>")
    txtstream.WriteLine("    <FitHeight>0</FitHeight>")
    txtstream.WriteLine("    <ValidPrinterInfo/>")
    txtstream.WriteLine("    <HorizontalResolution>600</HorizontalResolution>")
    txtstream.WriteLine("    <VerticalResolution>600</VerticalResolution>")
    txtstream.WriteLine("   </Print>")
    txtstream.WriteLine("   <Selected/>")
    txtstream.WriteLine("   <Panes>")
    txtstream.WriteLine("    <Pane>")
    txtstream.WriteLine("     <Number>3</Number>")
    txtstream.WriteLine("     <ActiveRow>9</ActiveRow>")
    txtstream.WriteLine("     <ActiveCol>7</ActiveCol>")
    txtstream.WriteLine("    </Pane>")
    txtstream.WriteLine("   </Panes>")
    txtstream.WriteLine("   <ProtectObjects>False</ProtectObjects>")
    txtstream.WriteLine("   <ProtectScenarios>False</ProtectScenarios>")
    txtstream.WriteLine("  </WorksheetOptions>")
    txtstream.WriteLine("</Worksheet>")
    txtstream.WriteLine("</Workbook>")
    txtstream.Close()
    ws.Run(ws.CurrentDirectory + "\\Products.xml")
```

CREATING XSL FILES

BELOW are examples of creating XSL files.

```
Set ws = CreateObject("WScript.Shell")
Set fso = CreateObject("Scripting.FileSystemObject")
Set txtstream =fso.OpenTextFile(ws.CurrentDirectory + "\Products.xsl", 2,
true, -2)
txtstream.WriteLine("<?xml version='1.0' encoding='UTF-8'?>")
txtstream.WriteLine("<xsl:stylesheet                    version='1.0'
xmlns:xsl='http://www.w3.org/1999/XSL/Transform'>")
txtstream.WriteLine("<xsl:template match=""/"">")
txtstream.WriteLine("<html>")
txtstream.WriteLine("<head>")
txtstream.WriteLine("<title>Products</title>")
txtstream.WriteLine("</head>")
#Add Stylesheet Here
txtstream.WriteLine("<body>")
rs.MoveFirst()
```

```
txtstream.WriteLine("<table border='0' Cellpadding='2' cellspacing='2'>")


txtstream.WriteLine("<tr>")
for x = 0 to rs.Fields.count-1
    txtstream.WriteLine("<th align='left' nowrap='true'>" + rs.Fields(x).Name
+ "</th>")
    Next
```

```
txtstream.WriteLine("</tr>")
txtstream.WriteLine("<tr>")
for x = 0 to rs.Fields.count-1
```

NONE

```
       txtstream.WriteLine("<td><xsl:value-of          select=""data/Products/"          +
rs.Fields(x).Name + """/></td>")
```

BUTTON

```
        txtstream.WriteLine("<td             align='left'    nowrap='true'><button
style='width:100%;'><xsl:value-of select=""data/Products/" + rs.Fields(x).Name   +
"""/></button></td>")
```

COMBOBOX

```
        txtstream.WriteLine("<td                                       align='left'
nowrap='true'><select><option><xsl:attribute           name='value'><xsl:value-of
select=""data/Products/" + rs.Fields(x).Name  + """/></xsl:attribute><xsl:value-of
select=""data/Products/" + rs.Fields(x).Name + """/></option></select></td>")
```

DIV

```
        txtstream.WriteLine("<td   align='left' nowrap='true'><div><xsl:value-of
select=""data/Products/" + rs.Fields(x).Name + """/></div></td>")
```

LINK

```
        txtstream.WriteLine("<td       align='left'  nowrap='true'><a  href='"   +
rs.Fields(x).Value + "'><xsl:value-of select=""data/Products/" + rs.Fields(x).Name
+ """/></a></td>")
```

LISTBOX

```
        txtstream.WriteLine("<td         align='left'      nowrap='true'><select
multiple><option><xsl:attribute                        name='value'><xsl:value-of
```

```
select=""""data/Products/" + rs.Fields(x).Name  + """"/></xsl:attribute><xsl:value-of
select=""""data/Products/" + rs.Fields(x).Name  + """"/></option></select></td>")
```

SPAN

```
        txtstream.WriteLine("<td   align='left' nowrap='true'><span><xsl:value-
of select=""""data/Products/" + rs.Fields(x).Name  + """"/></span></td>")
```

TEXTAREA

```
        txtstream.WriteLine("<td                              align='left'
nowrap='true'><textarea><xsl:value-of          select=""""data/Products/"      +
rs.Fields(x).Name  + """"/></textarea></td>")
```

TEXTBOX

```
        txtstream.WriteLine("<td         align='left'      nowrap='true'><input
type='text'><xsl:attribute name=""""value""""><xsl:value-of select=""""data/Products/"
+ rs.Fields(x).Name  + """"/></xsl:attribute></input></td>")
    Next
    txtstream.WriteLine("</tr>")
    txtstream.WriteLine("</table>")
    txtstream.WriteLine("</body>")
    txtstream.WriteLine("</html>")
    txtstream.WriteLine("</xsl:template>")
    txtstream.WriteLine("</xsl:stylesheet>")
    txtstream.Close()
```

MULTI LINE HORIZONTAL REPORTS

```
txtstream.WriteLine("<table border='0' Cellpadding='2' cellspacing='2>")


    txtstream.WriteLine("<tr>")
    for x = 0 to rs.Fields.count-1
```

```
        txtstream.WriteLine("<th>" + rs.Fields(x).Name + "</th>")
    Next
    txtstream.WriteLine("</tr>")
    txtstream.WriteLine("<xsl:for-each select=""data/Products"">")
    txtstream.WriteLine("<tr>")
    for x = 0 to rs.Fields.count-1
        txtstream.WriteLine("<td><xsl:value-of select="" " + rs.Fields(x).Name + "
""/></td>")
```

NONE

```
        txtstream.WriteLine("<td><xsl:value-of select=""" + rs.Fields(x).Name +
"""/></td>")
```

BUTTON

```
        txtstream.WriteLine("<td            align='left'    nowrap='true'><button
style='width:100%;'><xsl:value-of    select=""" +    rs.Fields(x).Name    +
"""/></button></td>")
```
COMBOBOX

```
        txtstream.WriteLine("<td                              align='left'
nowrap='true'><select><option><xsl:attribute            name='value'><xsl:value-of
select=""" +    rs.Fields(x).Name    +    """/></xsl:attribute><xsl:value-of
select=""data/Products/" + rs.Fields(x).Name + """/></option></select></td>")
```

DIV

```
        txtstream.WriteLine("<td   align='left' nowrap='true'><div><xsl:value-of
select=""data/Products/" + rs.Fields(x).Name + """/></div></td>")
```

LINK

```
        txtstream.WriteLine("<td      align='left'  nowrap='true'><a  href='" +
rs.Fields(x).Value + "'><xsl:value-of select=""data/Products/" + rs.Fields(x).Name
+ """/></a></td>")
```

LISTBOX

```
        txtstream.WriteLine("<td          align='left'      nowrap='true'><select
multiple><option><xsl:attribute                    name='value'><xsl:value-of
select=""data/Products/" + rs.Fields(x).Name  + """/></xsl:attribute><xsl:value-of
select=""data/Products/" + rs.Fields(x).Name  + """/></option></select></td>")
```

SPAN

```
        txtstream.WriteLine("<td   align='left' nowrap='true'><span><xsl:value-
of select=""data/Products/" + rs.Fields(x).Name  + """/></span></td>")
```

TEXTAREA

```
        txtstream.WriteLine("<td                                align='left'
nowrap='true'><textarea><xsl:value-of        select=""data/Products/"        +
rs.Fields(x).Name  + """/></textarea></td>")
```

TEXTBOX

```
        txtstream.WriteLine("<td          align='left'     nowrap='true'><input
type='text'><xsl:attribute name=""value""><xsl:value-of select=""data/Products/"
+ rs.Fields(x).Name  + """/></xsl:attribute></input></td>")
    Next
    txtstream.WriteLine("</tr>")
    txtstream.WriteLine("</xsl:for-each>")
    txtstream.WriteLine("</table>")
    txtstream.WriteLine("</body>")
    txtstream.WriteLine("</html>")
    txtstream.WriteLine("</xsl:template>")
    txtstream.WriteLine("</xsl:stylesheet>")
    txtstream.Close()
```

SINGLE LINE VERTICAL REPORTS

```
    for x = 0 to rs.Fields.count-1
        txtstream.WriteLine("<tr><th>" + rs.Fields(x).Name + "</th>")
```

NONE

```
txtstream.WriteLine("<td><xsl:value-of     select=""""data/Products/" +
rs.Fields(x).Name + """"/></td></tr>")
```

BUTTON

```
txtstream.WriteLine("<td        align='left'    nowrap='true'><button
style='width:100%;'><xsl:value-of select=""""data/Products/" + rs.Fields(x).Name +
""""/></button></td></tr>")
```

COMBOBOX

```
txtstream.WriteLine("<td                              align='left'
nowrap='true'><select><option><xsl:attribute        name='value'><xsl:value-of
select=""""data/Products/" + rs.Fields(x).Name + """"/></xsl:attribute><xsl:value-of
select=""""data/Products/"        +       rs.Fields(x).Name              +
""""/></option></select></td></tr>")
```

DIV

```
txtstream.WriteLine("<td   align='left' nowrap='true'><div><xsl:value-of
select=""""data/Products/" + rs.Fields(x).Name + """"/></div></td></tr>")
```

LINK

```
txtstream.WriteLine("<td        align='left'  nowrap='true'><a   href='" +
rs.Fields(x).Value + "'><xsl:value-of select=""""data/Products/" + rs.Fields(x).Name
+ """"/></a></td></tr>")
```

LISTBOX

```
txtstream.WriteLine("<td              align='left'     nowrap='true'><select
multiple><option><xsl:attribute               name='value'><xsl:value-of
select=""""data/Products/" + rs.Fields(x).Name + """"/></xsl:attribute><xsl:value-of
select=""""data/Products/"        +        rs.Fields(x).Name              +
""""/></option></select></td></tr>")
```

SPAN

```
        txtstream.WriteLine("<td   align='left' nowrap='true'><span><xsl:value-
of select=""data/Products/" + rs.Fields(x).Name + """/></span></td></tr>")
```

TEXTAREA

```
        txtstream.WriteLine("<td                                    align='left'
nowrap='true'><textarea><xsl:value-of        select=""data/Products/"       +
rs.Fields(x).Name  + """/></textarea></td></tr>")
```

TEXTBOX

```
        txtstream.WriteLine("<td          align='left'       nowrap='true'><input
type='text'><xsl:attribute  name=""value""><xsl:value-of select=""data/Products/"
+ rs.Fields(x).Name  + """/></xsl:attribute></input></td></tr>")

    Next
    txtstream.WriteLine("</table>")
    txtstream.WriteLine("</body>")
    txtstream.WriteLine("</html>")
    txtstream.WriteLine("</xsl:template>")
    txtstream.WriteLine("</xsl:stylesheet>")
    txtstream.Close()
```

MULTI LINE VERTICAL REPORTS

```
    txtstream.WriteLine("<table border='0' Cellpadding='2' cellspacing='2>")



    for x = 0 to rs.Fields.count-1
        txtstream.WriteLine("<tr><th        align='left'       nowrap='true'>"       +
rs.Fields(x).Name + "</th>")
```

NONE

```
txtstream.WriteLine("<xsl:for-each        select=""data/Products"""><td
align='left' nowrap='true'><xsl:value-of select="""" + rs.Fields(x).Name +
"""/></td></xsl:for-each></tr>")
```

BUTTON

```
txtstream.WriteLine("<xsl:for-each        select=""data/Products"""><td
align='left' nowrap='true'><button style='width:100%;'><xsl:value-of select="""" +
rs.Fields(x).Name + """/></button></td></xsl:for-each></tr>")
```

COMBOBOX

```
txtstream.WriteLine("<xsl:for-each        select=""data/Products"""><td
align='left'                    nowrap='true'><select><option><xsl:attribute
name='value'><xsl:value-of      select=""""      +      rs.Fields(x).Name      +
"""/></xsl:attribute><xsl:value-of select=""data/Products/" + rs.Fields(x).Name +
"""/></option></select></td></xsl:for-each></tr>")
```

DIV

```
txtstream.WriteLine("<xsl:for-each        select=""data/Products"""><td
align='left'   nowrap='true'><div><xsl:value-of   select=""data/Products/"   +
rs.Fields(x).Name + """/></div></td></xsl:for-each></tr>")
```

LINK

```
txtstream.WriteLine("<xsl:for-each        select=""data/Products"""><td
align='left' nowrap='true'><a href='" + rs.Fields(x).Value + "'><xsl:value-of
select=""data/Products/"   +   rs.Fields(x).Name   +   """/></a></td></xsl:for-
each></tr>")
```

LISTBOX

```
txtstream.WriteLine("<xsl:for-each        select=""data/Products"""><td
align='left'            nowrap='true'><select          multiple><option><xsl:attribute
name='value'><xsl:value-of  select=""data/Products/"  +  rs.Fields(x).Name      +
```

```
"""/></xsl:attribute><xsl:value-of select=""""data/Products/" + rs.Fields(x).Name +
"""/></option></select></td></xsl:for-each></tr>")
```

SPAN

```
        txtstream.WriteLine("<xsl:for-each        select=""""data/Products"""><td
align='left'   nowrap='true'><span><xsl:value-of   select=""""data/Products/"   +
rs.Fields(x).Name + """/></span></td></xsl:for-each></tr>")
```

TEXTAREA

```
        txtstream.WriteLine("<xsl:for-each        select=""""data/Products"""><td
align='left'  nowrap='true'><textarea><xsl:value-of  select=""""data/Products/"  +
rs.Fields(x).Name + """/></textarea></td></xsl:for-each></tr>")
```

TEXTBOX

```
        txtstream.WriteLine("<xsl:for-each        select=""""data/Products"""><td
align='left'           nowrap='true'><input          type='text'><xsl:attribute
name=""""value""""><xsl:value-of select=""""data/Products/" + rs.Fields(x).Name +
"""/></xsl:attribute></input></td></xsl:for-each></tr>")
```

```
    Next
    txtstream.WriteLine("</table>")
    txtstream.WriteLine("</body>")
    txtstream.WriteLine("</html>")
    txtstream.WriteLine("</xsl:template>")
    txtstream.WriteLine("</xsl:stylesheet>")
    txtstream.Close()
```

SINGLE LINE HORIZONTAL TABLES

```
    txtstream.WriteLine("<table        style='border:Double;border-width:1px;border-
    color:navy;' rules=all frames=both cellpadding=2 cellspacing=2 Width=0>")
```

```
    txtstream.WriteLine("<tr>")
```

```
for x = 0 to rs.Fields.count-1
     txtstream.WriteLine("<th align='left' nowrap='true'>" + rs.Fields(x).Name
+ "</th>")

     txtstream.WriteLine("</tr>")
     txtstream.WriteLine("<tr>")
     for x = 0 to rs.Fields.count-1
```

NONE

```
     txtstream.WriteLine("<td><xsl:value-of     select=""data/Products/"     +
rs.Fields(x).Name  + """/></td>")
```

BUTTON

```
     txtstream.WriteLine("<td          align='left'     nowrap='true'><button
style='width:100%;'><xsl:value-of select=""data/Products/" + rs.Fields(x).Name  +
"""/></button></td>")
```

COMBOBOX

```
     txtstream.WriteLine("<td                                    align='left'
nowrap='true'><select><option><xsl:attribute          name='value'><xsl:value-of
select=""data/Products/" + rs.Fields(x).Name  + """/></xsl:attribute><xsl:value-of
select=""data/Products/" + rs.Fields(x).Name  + """/></option></select></td>")
```

DIV

```
     txtstream.WriteLine("<td   align='left'  nowrap='true'><div><xsl:value-of
select=""data/Products/" + rs.Fields(x).Name  + """/></div></td>")
```

LINK

```
     txtstream.WriteLine("<td      align='left'   nowrap='true'><a  href='"   +
rs.Fields(x).Value + "'><xsl:value-of select=""data/Products/" + rs.Fields(x).Name
+ """/></a></td>")
```

LISTBOX

```
        txtstream.WriteLine("<td          align='left'      nowrap='true'><select
multiple><option><xsl:attribute                          name='value'><xsl:value-of
select=""data/Products/" + rs.Fields(x).Name  + """/></xsl:attribute><xsl:value-of
select=""data/Products/" + rs.Fields(x).Name  + """/></option></select></td>")
```

SPAN

```
        txtstream.WriteLine("<td   align='left' nowrap='true'><span><xsl:value-
of select=""data/Products/" + rs.Fields(x).Name  + """/></span></td>")
```

TEXTAREA

```
        txtstream.WriteLine("<td                                   align='left'
nowrap='true'><textarea><xsl:value-of         select=""data/Products/"          +
rs.Fields(x).Name  + """/></textarea></td>")
```

TEXTBOX

```
        txtstream.WriteLine("<td          align='left'      nowrap='true'><input
type='text'><xsl:attribute  name=""value""><xsl:value-of  select=""data/Products/"
+ rs.Fields(x).Name  + """/></xsl:attribute></input></td>")
```

```
    Next
    txtstream.WriteLine("</tr>")
    txtstream.WriteLine("</table>")
    txtstream.WriteLine("</body>")
    txtstream.WriteLine("</html>")
    txtstream.WriteLine("</xsl:template>")
    txtstream.WriteLine("</xsl:stylesheet>")
    txtstream.Close()
```

MULTI LINE HORIZONTAL TABLES

```
    txtstream.WriteLine("<table        style='border:Double;border-width:1px;border-
color:navy;' rules=all frames=both cellpadding=2 cellspacing=2 Width=0>")
```

```
txtstream.WriteLine("<tr>")
for x = 0 to rs.Fields.count-1
   txtstream.WriteLine("<th>" + rs.Fields(x).Name + "</th>")
Next
txtstream.WriteLine("</tr>")
txtstream.WriteLine("<xsl:for-each select=""data/Products"">")
txtstream.WriteLine("<tr>")
for x = 0 to rs.Fields.count-1
   txtstream.WriteLine("<td><xsl:value-of select="" " + rs.Fields(x).Name + "
""/></td>")
```

NONE

```
txtstream.WriteLine("<td><xsl:value-of select=""" + rs.Fields(x).Name +
"""/></td>")
```

BUTTON

```
txtstream.WriteLine("<td          align='left'     nowrap='true'><button
style='width:100%;'><xsl:value-of    select="""   +   rs.Fields(x).Name     +
"""/></button></td>")
```

COMBOBOX

```
txtstream.WriteLine("<td                                 align='left'
nowrap='true'><select><option><xsl:attribute          name='value'><xsl:value-of
select="""    +    rs.Fields(x).Name       +    """/></xsl:attribute><xsl:value-of
select=""data/Products/" + rs.Fields(x).Name + """/></option></select></td>")
```

DIV

```
txtstream.WriteLine("<td   align='left'  nowrap='true'><div><xsl:value-of
select=""data/Products/" + rs.Fields(x).Name + """/></div></td>")
```

LINK

```
        txtstream.WriteLine("<td      align='left'  nowrap='true'><a href='" +
rs.Fields(x).Value + "'><xsl:value-of select=""data/Products/" + rs.Fields(x).Name
+ """/></a></td>")
```

LISTBOX

```
        txtstream.WriteLine("<td       align='left'     nowrap='true'><select
multiple><option><xsl:attribute            name='value'><xsl:value-of
select=""data/Products/" + rs.Fields(x).Name  + """/></xsl:attribute><xsl:value-of
select=""data/Products/" + rs.Fields(x).Name  + """/></option></select></td>")
```

SPAN

```
        txtstream.WriteLine("<td   align='left' nowrap='true'><span><xsl:value-
of select=""data/Products/" + rs.Fields(x).Name  + """/></span></td>")
```

TEXTAREA

```
        txtstream.WriteLine("<td                             align='left'
nowrap='true'><textarea><xsl:value-of       select=""data/Products/"       +
rs.Fields(x).Name  + """/></textarea></td>")
```

TEXTBOX

```
        txtstream.WriteLine("<td       align='left'    nowrap='true'><input
type='text'><xsl:attribute name=""value""><xsl:value-of select=""data/Products/"
+ rs.Fields(x).Name  + """/></xsl:attribute></input></td>")

    Next
    txtstream.WriteLine("</tr>")
    txtstream.WriteLine("</xsl:for-each>")
    txtstream.WriteLine("</table>")
    txtstream.WriteLine("</body>")
    txtstream.WriteLine("</html>")
    txtstream.WriteLine("</xsl:template>")
    txtstream.WriteLine("</xsl:stylesheet>")
    txtstream.Close()
```

```
for x = 0 to rs.Fields.count-1
    txtstream.WriteLine("<tr><th>" + rs.Fields(x).Name + "</th>")
```

NONE

```
txtstream.WriteLine("<td><xsl:value-of     select=""data/Products/" +
rs.Fields(x).Name  + """/></td></tr>")
```

BUTTON

```
txtstream.WriteLine("<td          align='left'     nowrap='true'><button
style='width:100%;'><xsl:value-of select=""data/Products/" + rs.Fields(x).Name +
"""/></button></td></tr>")
```

COMBOBOX

```
txtstream.WriteLine("<td                                align='left'
nowrap='true'><select><option><xsl:attribute          name='value'><xsl:value-of
select=""data/Products/" + rs.Fields(x).Name  + """/></xsl:attribute><xsl:value-of
select=""data/Products/"        +       rs.Fields(x).Name                +
"""/></option></select></td></tr>")
```

DIV

```
txtstream.WriteLine("<td   align='left' nowrap='true'><div><xsl:value-of
select=""data/Products/" + rs.Fields(x).Name  + """/></div></td></tr>")
```

LINK

```
txtstream.WriteLine("<td      align='left' nowrap='true'><a   href='" +
rs.Fields(x).Value  + "'><xsl:value-of select=""data/Products/" + rs.Fields(x).Name
+ """/></a></td></tr>")
```

LISTBOX

```
        txtstream.WriteLine("<td          align='left'       nowrap='true'><select
multiple><option><xsl:attribute                        name='value'><xsl:value-of
select=""data/Products/" + rs.Fields(x).Name + """/></xsl:attribute><xsl:value-of
select=""data/Products/"        +         rs.Fields(x).Name                +
"""/></option></select></td></tr>")
```

SPAN

```
        txtstream.WriteLine("<td  align='left' nowrap='true'><span><xsl:value-
of select=""data/Products/" + rs.Fields(x).Name + """/></span></td></tr>")
```

TEXTAREA

```
        txtstream.WriteLine("<td                                   align='left'
nowrap='true'><textarea><xsl:value-of         select=""data/Products/"      +
rs.Fields(x).Name + """/></textarea></td></tr>")
```

TEXTBOX

```
        txtstream.WriteLine("<td          align='left'     nowrap='true'><input
type='text'><xsl:attribute name=""value""><xsl:value-of select=""data/Products/"
+ rs.Fields(x).Name + """/></xsl:attribute></input></td></tr>")
```

```
    Next
    txtstream.WriteLine("</table>")
    txtstream.WriteLine("</body>")
    txtstream.WriteLine("</html>")
    txtstream.WriteLine("</xsl:template>")
    txtstream.WriteLine("</xsl:stylesheet>")
    txtstream.Close()
```

MULTI LINE VERTICAL TABLES

```
    txtstream.WriteLine("<table       style='border:Double;border-width:1px;border-
color:navy;' rules=all frames=both cellpadding=2 cellspacing=2 Width=0>")
```

```
for x = 0 to rs.Fields.count-1
        txtstream.WriteLine("<tr><th        align='left'        nowrap='true'>"        +
rs.Fields(x).Name + "</th>")
```

NONE

```
        txtstream.WriteLine("<xsl:for-each            select=""data/Products""><td
align='left'  nowrap='true'><xsl:value-of  select="""  +  rs.Fields(x).Name  +
"""/></td></xsl:for-each></tr>")
```

BUTTON

```
        txtstream.WriteLine("<xsl:for-each            select=""data/Products""><td
align='left' nowrap='true'><button style='width:100%;'><xsl:value-of select=""" +
rs.Fields(x).Name + """/></button></td></xsl:for-each></tr>")
```

COMBOBOX

```
        txtstream.WriteLine("<xsl:for-each            select=""data/Products""><td
align='left'                              nowrap='true'><select><option><xsl:attribute
name='value'><xsl:value-of      select="""      +      rs.Fields(x).Name      +
"""/></xsl:attribute><xsl:value-of select=""data/Products/" + rs.Fields(x).Name +
"""/></option></select></td></xsl:for-each></tr>")
```

DIV

```
        txtstream.WriteLine("<xsl:for-each            select=""data/Products""><td
align='left'    nowrap='true'><div><xsl:value-of    select=""data/Products/"    +
rs.Fields(x).Name + """/></div></td></xsl:for-each></tr>")
```

LINK

```
        txtstream.WriteLine("<xsl:for-each            select=""data/Products""><td
align='left'  nowrap='true'><a  href='"  +  rs.Fields(x).Value  +  "'><xsl:value-of
```

```
select="""data/Products/"  +  rs.Fields(x).Name  +  """"/></a></td></xsl:for-
each></tr>")
```

LISTBOX

```
        txtstream.WriteLine("<xsl:for-each        select="""data/Products""><td
align='left'        nowrap='true'><select        multiple><option><xsl:attribute
name='value'><xsl:value-of  select="""data/Products/"  +  rs.Fields(x).Name  +
""""/></xsl:attribute><xsl:value-of select="""data/Products/" + rs.Fields(x).Name  +
""""/></option></select></td></xsl:for-each></tr>")
```

SPAN

```
        txtstream.WriteLine("<xsl:for-each        select="""data/Products""><td
align='left'  nowrap='true'><span><xsl:value-of  select="""data/Products/"  +
rs.Fields(x).Name + """"/></span></td></xsl:for-each></tr>")
```

TEXTAREA

```
        txtstream.WriteLine("<xsl:for-each        select="""data/Products""><td
align='left'  nowrap='true'><textarea><xsl:value-of  select="""data/Products/"  +
rs.Fields(x).Name + """"/></textarea></td></xsl:for-each></tr>")
```

TEXTBOX

```
        txtstream.WriteLine("<xsl:for-each        select="""data/Products""><td
align='left'            nowrap='true'><input            type='text'><xsl:attribute
name="""value"""><xsl:value-of  select="""data/Products/"  +  rs.Fields(x).Name  +
""""/></xsl:attribute></input></td></xsl:for-each></tr>")

    Next
    txtstream.WriteLine("</table>")
    txtstream.WriteLine("</body>")
    txtstream.WriteLine("</html>")
    txtstream.WriteLine("</xsl:template>")
    txtstream.WriteLine("</xsl:stylesheet>")
    txtstream.Close()
```

STYLESHEETS

Add some Pizzazz To your ASP, HTA, HTML and XSL pages

CSS turns okay into Amazing

BELOW is an assortment of stylesheets. There is nothing spectacular about them   Just some ideas you can modify and put your own twist on them.

```
txtstream.WriteLine("<style type='text/css'>")
txtstream.WriteLine("th")
txtstream.WriteLine("{")
txtstream.WriteLine("   COLOR: Black;")
txtstream.WriteLine("}")
txtstream.WriteLine("td")
txtstream.WriteLine("{")
txtstream.WriteLine("   COLOR: Black;")
txtstream.WriteLine("}")
txtstream.WriteLine("</style>")
```

ITS A TABLE

```
txtstream.WriteLine("<style type='text/css'>")
txtstream.WriteLine("#itsthetable {")
txtstream.WriteLine("        font-family: Georgia, ""Times New Roman"", Times, serif;")
txtstream.WriteLine("        color: #036;")
txtstream.WriteLine("}")
txtstream.WriteLine("caption {")
txtstream.WriteLine("        font-size: 48px;")
txtstream.WriteLine("        color: #036;")
txtstream.WriteLine("        font-weight: bolder;")
txtstream.WriteLine("        font-variant: small-caps;")
txtstream.WriteLine("}")
txtstream.WriteLine("th {")
txtstream.WriteLine("        font-size: 12px;")
txtstream.WriteLine("        color: #FFF;")
txtstream.WriteLine("        background-color: #06C;")
txtstream.WriteLine("        padding: 8px 4px;")
txtstream.WriteLine("        border-bottom: 1px solid #015ebc;")
txtstream.WriteLine("}")
txtstream.WriteLine("table {")
txtstream.WriteLine("        margin: 0;")
txtstream.WriteLine("        padding: 0;")
txtstream.WriteLine("        border-collapse: collapse;")
```

```
txtstream.WriteLine("          border: 1px solid #06C;")
txtstream.WriteLine("          width: 100%")
txtstream.WriteLine("}")
txtstream.WriteLine("#itsthetable th a:link, #itsthetable th a:visited {")
txtstream.WriteLine("          color: #FFF;")
txtstream.WriteLine("          text-decoration: none;")
txtstream.WriteLine("          border-left: 5px solid #FFF;")
txtstream.WriteLine("          padding-left: 3px;")
txtstream.WriteLine("}")
txtstream.WriteLine("th a:hover, #itsthetable th a:active {")
txtstream.WriteLine("          color: #F90;")
txtstream.WriteLine("          text-decoration: line-through;")
txtstream.WriteLine("          border-left: 5px solid #F90;")
txtstream.WriteLine("          padding-left: 3px;")
txtstream.WriteLine("}")
txtstream.WriteLine("tbody th:hover {")
txtstream.WriteLine("          background-image:
url(imgs/tbody_hover.gif);")
txtstream.WriteLine("          background-position: bottom;")
txtstream.WriteLine("          background-repeat: repeat-x;")
txtstream.WriteLine("}")
txtstream.WriteLine("td {")
txtstream.WriteLine("          background-color: #f2f2f2;")
txtstream.WriteLine("          padding: 4px;")
txtstream.WriteLine("          font-size: 12px;")
txtstream.WriteLine("}")
txtstream.WriteLine("#itsthetable td:hover {")
txtstream.WriteLine("          background-color: #f8f8f8;")
txtstream.WriteLine("}")
txtstream.WriteLine("#itsthetable td a:link, #itsthetable td a:visited {")
txtstream.WriteLine("          color: #039;")
txtstream.WriteLine("          text-decoration: none;")
txtstream.WriteLine("          border-left: 3px solid #039;")
txtstream.WriteLine("          padding-left: 3px;")
txtstream.WriteLine("}")
txtstream.WriteLine("#itsthetable td a:hover, #itsthetable td a:active {")
txtstream.WriteLine("          color: #06C;")
txtstream.WriteLine("          text-decoration: line-through;")
txtstream.WriteLine("          border-left: 3px solid #06C;")
txtstream.WriteLine("          padding-left: 3px;")
```

```
txtstream.WriteLine("}")
txtstream.WriteLine("#itsthetable th {")
txtstream.WriteLine("          text-align: left;")
txtstream.WriteLine("          width: 150px;")
txtstream.WriteLine("}")
txtstream.WriteLine("#itsthetable tr {")
txtstream.WriteLine("          border-bottom: 1px solid #CCC;")
txtstream.WriteLine("}")
txtstream.WriteLine("#itsthetable thead th {")
txtstream.WriteLine("          background-image: url(imgs/thead_back.gif);")
txtstream.WriteLine("          background-repeat: repeat-x;")
txtstream.WriteLine("          background-color: #06C;")
txtstream.WriteLine("          height: 30px;")
txtstream.WriteLine("          font-size: 18px;")
txtstream.WriteLine("          text-align: center;")
txtstream.WriteLine("          text-shadow: #333 2px 2px;")
txtstream.WriteLine("          border: 2px;")
txtstream.WriteLine("}")
txtstream.WriteLine("#itsthetable tfoot th {")
txtstream.WriteLine("          background-image: url(imgs/tfoot_back.gif);")
txtstream.WriteLine("          background-repeat: repeat-x;")
txtstream.WriteLine("          background-color: #036;")
txtstream.WriteLine("          height: 30px;")
txtstream.WriteLine("          font-size: 28px;")
txtstream.WriteLine("          text-align: center;")
txtstream.WriteLine("          text-shadow: #333 2px 2px;")
txtstream.WriteLine("}")
txtstream.WriteLine("#itsthetable tfoot td {")
txtstream.WriteLine("          background-image: url(imgs/tfoot_back.gif);")
txtstream.WriteLine("          background-repeat: repeat-x;")
txtstream.WriteLine("          background-color: #036;")
txtstream.WriteLine("          color: FFF;")
txtstream.WriteLine("          height: 30px;")
txtstream.WriteLine("          font-size: 24px;")
txtstream.WriteLine("          text-align: left;")
txtstream.WriteLine("          text-shadow: #333 2px 2px;")
txtstream.WriteLine("}")
txtstream.WriteLine("tbody td a(href=""http://www.csslab.cl/"") {")
txtstream.WriteLine("          font-weight: bolder;")
txtstream.WriteLine("}")
```

```
txtstream.WriteLine("</style>")
```

```
txtstream.WriteLine("<style type='text/css'>")
txtstream.WriteLine("th")
txtstream.WriteLine("{")
txtstream.WriteLine("   COLOR: white;")
txtstream.WriteLine("   BACKGROUND-COLOR: black;")
txtstream.WriteLine("   FONT-FAMILY: Cambria, serif;")
txtstream.WriteLine("   FONT-SIZE: 12px;")
txtstream.WriteLine("   text-align: left;")
txtstream.WriteLine("   white-Space: nowrap='nowrap';")
txtstream.WriteLine("}")
txtstream.WriteLine("td")
txtstream.WriteLine("{")
txtstream.WriteLine("   COLOR: white;")
txtstream.WriteLine("   BACKGROUND-COLOR: black;")
txtstream.WriteLine("   FONT-FAMILY: font-family: Cambria, serif;")
txtstream.WriteLine("   FONT-SIZE: 12px;")
txtstream.WriteLine("   text-align: left;")
txtstream.WriteLine("   white-Space: nowrap='nowrap';")
txtstream.WriteLine("}")
txtstream.WriteLine("div")
txtstream.WriteLine("{")
txtstream.WriteLine("   COLOR: white;")
txtstream.WriteLine("   BACKGROUND-COLOR: black;")
txtstream.WriteLine("   FONT-FAMILY: font-family: Cambria, serif;")
txtstream.WriteLine("   FONT-SIZE: 10px;")
txtstream.WriteLine("   text-align: left;")
txtstream.WriteLine("   white-Space: nowrap='nowrap';")
txtstream.WriteLine("}")
txtstream.WriteLine("span")
txtstream.WriteLine("{")
txtstream.WriteLine("   COLOR: white;")
txtstream.WriteLine("   BACKGROUND-COLOR: black;")
txtstream.WriteLine("   FONT-FAMILY: font-family: Cambria, serif;")
txtstream.WriteLine("   FONT-SIZE: 10px;")
```

```
txtstream.WriteLine("    text-align: left;")
txtstream.WriteLine("    white-Space: nowrap='nowrap';")
txtstream.WriteLine("    display:inline-block;")
txtstream.WriteLine("    width: 100%;")
txtstream.WriteLine("}")
txtstream.WriteLine("textarea")
txtstream.WriteLine("{")
txtstream.WriteLine("    COLOR: white;")
txtstream.WriteLine("    BACKGROUND-COLOR: black;")
txtstream.WriteLine("    FONT-FAMILY: font-family: Cambria, serif;")
txtstream.WriteLine("    FONT-SIZE: 10px;")
txtstream.WriteLine("    text-align: left;")
txtstream.WriteLine("    white-Space: nowrap='nowrap';")
txtstream.WriteLine("    width: 100%;")
txtstream.WriteLine("}")
txtstream.WriteLine("select")
txtstream.WriteLine("{")
txtstream.WriteLine("    COLOR: white;")
txtstream.WriteLine("    BACKGROUND-COLOR: black;")
txtstream.WriteLine("    FONT-FAMILY: font-family: Cambria, serif;")
txtstream.WriteLine("    FONT-SIZE: 10px;")
txtstream.WriteLine("    text-align: left;")
txtstream.WriteLine("    white-Space: nowrap='nowrap';")
txtstream.WriteLine("    width: 100%;")
txtstream.WriteLine("}")
txtstream.WriteLine("input")
txtstream.WriteLine("{")
txtstream.WriteLine("    COLOR: white;")
txtstream.WriteLine("    BACKGROUND-COLOR: black;")
txtstream.WriteLine("    FONT-FAMILY: font-family: Cambria, serif;")
txtstream.WriteLine("    FONT-SIZE: 12px;")
txtstream.WriteLine("    text-align: left;")
txtstream.WriteLine("    display:table-cell;")
txtstream.WriteLine("    white-Space: nowrap='nowrap';")
txtstream.WriteLine("}")
txtstream.WriteLine("h1 {")
txtstream.WriteLine("color: antiquewhite;")
txtstream.WriteLine("text-shadow: 1px 1px 1px black;")
txtstream.WriteLine("padding: 3px;")
txtstream.WriteLine("text-align: center;")
```

```
txtstream.WriteLine("box-shadow: in2px 2px 5px rgba(0,0,0,0.5), in-2px -
2px 5px rgba(255,255,255,0.5);")
txtstream.WriteLine("}")
txtstream.WriteLine("</style>")
```

COLORED TEXT

```
txtstream.WriteLine("<style type='text/css'>")
txtstream.WriteLine("th")
txtstream.WriteLine("{")
txtstream.WriteLine("   COLOR: darkred;")
txtstream.WriteLine("   BACKGROUND-COLOR: #eeeeee;")
txtstream.WriteLine("   FONT-FAMILY: Cambria, serif;")
txtstream.WriteLine("   FONT-SIZE: 12px;")
txtstream.WriteLine("   text-align: left;")
txtstream.WriteLine("   white-Space: nowrap='nowrap';")
txtstream.WriteLine("}")
txtstream.WriteLine("td")
txtstream.WriteLine("{")
txtstream.WriteLine("   COLOR: navy;")
txtstream.WriteLine("   BACKGROUND-COLOR: #eeeeee;")
txtstream.WriteLine("   FONT-FAMILY: font-family: Cambria, serif;")
txtstream.WriteLine("   FONT-SIZE: 12px;")
txtstream.WriteLine("   text-align: left;")
txtstream.WriteLine("   white-Space: nowrap='nowrap';")
txtstream.WriteLine("}")
txtstream.WriteLine("div")
txtstream.WriteLine("{")
txtstream.WriteLine("   COLOR: white;")
txtstream.WriteLine("   BACKGROUND-COLOR: navy;")
txtstream.WriteLine("   FONT-FAMILY: font-family: Cambria, serif;")
txtstream.WriteLine("   FONT-SIZE: 10px;")
txtstream.WriteLine("   text-align: left;")
txtstream.WriteLine("   white-Space: nowrap='nowrap';")
txtstream.WriteLine("}")
txtstream.WriteLine("span")
txtstream.WriteLine("{")
txtstream.WriteLine("   COLOR: white;")
```

```
txtstream.WriteLine("   BACKGROUND-COLOR: navy;")
txtstream.WriteLine("   FONT-FAMILY: font-family: Cambria, serif;")
txtstream.WriteLine("   FONT-SIZE: 10px;")
txtstream.WriteLine("   text-align: left;")
txtstream.WriteLine("   white-Space: nowrap='nowrap';")
txtstream.WriteLine("   display:inline-block;")
txtstream.WriteLine("   width: 100%;")
txtstream.WriteLine("}")
txtstream.WriteLine("textarea")
txtstream.WriteLine("{")
txtstream.WriteLine("   COLOR: white;")
txtstream.WriteLine("   BACKGROUND-COLOR: navy;")
txtstream.WriteLine("   FONT-FAMILY: font-family: Cambria, serif;")
txtstream.WriteLine("   FONT-SIZE: 10px;")
txtstream.WriteLine("   text-align: left;")
txtstream.WriteLine("   white-Space: nowrap='nowrap';")
txtstream.WriteLine("   width: 100%;")
txtstream.WriteLine("}")
txtstream.WriteLine("select")
txtstream.WriteLine("{")
txtstream.WriteLine("   COLOR: white;")
txtstream.WriteLine("   BACKGROUND-COLOR: navy;")
txtstream.WriteLine("   FONT-FAMILY: font-family: Cambria, serif;")
txtstream.WriteLine("   FONT-SIZE: 10px;")
txtstream.WriteLine("   text-align: left;")
txtstream.WriteLine("   white-Space: nowrap='nowrap';")
txtstream.WriteLine("   width: 100%;")
txtstream.WriteLine("}")
txtstream.WriteLine("input")
txtstream.WriteLine("{")
txtstream.WriteLine("   COLOR: white;")
txtstream.WriteLine("   BACKGROUND-COLOR: navy;")
txtstream.WriteLine("   FONT-FAMILY: font-family: Cambria, serif;")
txtstream.WriteLine("   FONT-SIZE: 12px;")
txtstream.WriteLine("   text-align: left;")
txtstream.WriteLine("   display:table-cell;")
txtstream.WriteLine("   white-Space: nowrap='nowrap';")
txtstream.WriteLine("}")
txtstream.WriteLine("h1 {")
txtstream.WriteLine("color: antiquewhite;")
```

```
txtstream.WriteLine("text-shadow: 1px 1px 1px black;")
txtstream.WriteLine("padding: 3px;")
txtstream.WriteLine("text-align: center;")
txtstream.WriteLine("box-shadow: in2px 2px 5px rgba(0,0,0,0.5), in-2px -
2px 5px rgba(255,255,255,0.5);")
txtstream.WriteLine("}")
txtstream.WriteLine("</style>")
```

OSCILLATING ROW COLORS

```
txtstream.WriteLine("<style type='text/css'>")
txtstream.WriteLine("th")
txtstream.WriteLine("{")
txtstream.WriteLine("   COLOR: white;")
txtstream.WriteLine("   BACKGROUND-COLOR: navy;")
txtstream.WriteLine("   FONT-FAMILY: Cambria, serif;")
txtstream.WriteLine("   FONT-SIZE: 12px;")
txtstream.WriteLine("   text-align: left;")
txtstream.WriteLine("   white-Space: nowrap='nowrap';")
txtstream.WriteLine("}")
txtstream.WriteLine("td")
txtstream.WriteLine("{")
txtstream.WriteLine("   COLOR: navy;")
txtstream.WriteLine("   FONT-FAMILY: font-family: Cambria, serif;")
txtstream.WriteLine("   FONT-SIZE: 12px;")
txtstream.WriteLine("   text-align: left;")
txtstream.WriteLine("   white-Space: nowrap='nowrap';")
txtstream.WriteLine("}")
txtstream.WriteLine("div")
txtstream.WriteLine("{")
txtstream.WriteLine("   COLOR: navy;")
txtstream.WriteLine("   FONT-FAMILY: font-family: Cambria, serif;")
txtstream.WriteLine("   FONT-SIZE: 12px;")
txtstream.WriteLine("   text-align: left;")
txtstream.WriteLine("   white-Space: nowrap='nowrap';")
txtstream.WriteLine("}")
txtstream.WriteLine("span")
txtstream.WriteLine("{")
```

```
txtstream.WriteLine("    COLOR: navy;")
txtstream.WriteLine("    FONT-FAMILY: font-family: Cambria, serif;")
txtstream.WriteLine("    FONT-SIZE: 12px;")
txtstream.WriteLine("    text-align: left;")
txtstream.WriteLine("    white-Space: nowrap='nowrap';")
txtstream.WriteLine("    width: 100%;")
txtstream.WriteLine("}")
txtstream.WriteLine("textarea")
txtstream.WriteLine("{")
txtstream.WriteLine("    COLOR: navy;")
txtstream.WriteLine("    FONT-FAMILY: font-family: Cambria, serif;")
txtstream.WriteLine("    FONT-SIZE: 12px;")
txtstream.WriteLine("    text-align: left;")
txtstream.WriteLine("    white-Space: nowrap='nowrap';")
txtstream.WriteLine("    display:inline-block;")
txtstream.WriteLine("    width: 100%;")
txtstream.WriteLine("}")
txtstream.WriteLine("select")
txtstream.WriteLine("{")
txtstream.WriteLine("    COLOR: navy;")
txtstream.WriteLine("    FONT-FAMILY: font-family: Cambria, serif;")
txtstream.WriteLine("    FONT-SIZE: 10px;")
txtstream.WriteLine("    text-align: left;")
txtstream.WriteLine("    white-Space: nowrap='nowrap';")
txtstream.WriteLine("    display:inline-block;")
txtstream.WriteLine("    width: 100%;")
txtstream.WriteLine("}")
txtstream.WriteLine("input")
txtstream.WriteLine("{")
txtstream.WriteLine("    COLOR: navy;")
txtstream.WriteLine("    FONT-FAMILY: font-family: Cambria, serif;")
txtstream.WriteLine("    FONT-SIZE: 12px;")
txtstream.WriteLine("    text-align: left;")
txtstream.WriteLine("    display:table-cell;")
txtstream.WriteLine("    white-Space: nowrap='nowrap';")
txtstream.WriteLine("}")
txtstream.WriteLine("h1 {")
txtstream.WriteLine("color: antiquewhite;")
txtstream.WriteLine("text-shadow: 1px 1px 1px black;")
txtstream.WriteLine("padding: 3px;")
```

```
txtstream.WriteLine("text-align: center;")
txtstream.WriteLine("box-shadow: in2px 2px 5px rgba(0,0,0,0.5), in-2px -
2px 5px rgba(255,255,255,0.5);")
txtstream.WriteLine("}")
txtstream.WriteLine("tr:nth-child(even){background-color:#f2f2f2;}")
txtstream.WriteLine("tr:nth-child(odd){background-color:#cccccc;
color:#f2f2f2;}")
txtstream.WriteLine("</style>")
```

GHOST DECORATED

```
txtstream.WriteLine("<style type='text/css'>")
txtstream.WriteLine("th")
txtstream.WriteLine("{")
txtstream.WriteLine("   COLOR: black;")
txtstream.WriteLine("   BACKGROUND-COLOR: white;")
txtstream.WriteLine("   FONT-FAMILY: Cambria, serif;")
txtstream.WriteLine("   FONT-SIZE: 12px;")
txtstream.WriteLine("   text-align: left;")
txtstream.WriteLine("   white-Space: nowrap='nowrap';")
txtstream.WriteLine("}")
txtstream.WriteLine("td")
txtstream.WriteLine("{")
txtstream.WriteLine("   COLOR: black;")
txtstream.WriteLine("   BACKGROUND-COLOR: white;")
txtstream.WriteLine("   FONT-FAMILY: font-family: Cambria, serif;")
txtstream.WriteLine("   FONT-SIZE: 12px;")
txtstream.WriteLine("   text-align: left;")
txtstream.WriteLine("   white-Space: nowrap='nowrap';")
txtstream.WriteLine("}")
txtstream.WriteLine("div")
txtstream.WriteLine("{")
txtstream.WriteLine("   COLOR: black;")
txtstream.WriteLine("   BACKGROUND-COLOR: white;")
txtstream.WriteLine("   FONT-FAMILY: font-family: Cambria, serif;")
txtstream.WriteLine("   FONT-SIZE: 10px;")
txtstream.WriteLine("   text-align: left;")
txtstream.WriteLine("   white-Space: nowrap='nowrap';")
```

```
txtstream.WriteLine("}")
txtstream.WriteLine("span")
txtstream.WriteLine("{")
txtstream.WriteLine("    COLOR: black;")
txtstream.WriteLine("    BACKGROUND-COLOR: white;")
txtstream.WriteLine("    FONT-FAMILY: font-family: Cambria, serif;")
txtstream.WriteLine("    FONT-SIZE: 10px;")
txtstream.WriteLine("    text-align: left;")
txtstream.WriteLine("    white-Space: nowrap='nowrap';")
txtstream.WriteLine("    display:inline-block;")
txtstream.WriteLine("    width: 100%;")
txtstream.WriteLine("}")
txtstream.WriteLine("textarea")
txtstream.WriteLine("{")
txtstream.WriteLine("    COLOR: black;")
txtstream.WriteLine("    BACKGROUND-COLOR: white;")
txtstream.WriteLine("    FONT-FAMILY: font-family: Cambria, serif;")
txtstream.WriteLine("    FONT-SIZE: 10px;")
txtstream.WriteLine("    text-align: left;")
txtstream.WriteLine("    white-Space: nowrap='nowrap';")
txtstream.WriteLine("    width: 100%;")
txtstream.WriteLine("}")
txtstream.WriteLine("select")
txtstream.WriteLine("{")
txtstream.WriteLine("    COLOR: black;")
txtstream.WriteLine("    BACKGROUND-COLOR: white;")
txtstream.WriteLine("    FONT-FAMILY: font-family: Cambria, serif;")
txtstream.WriteLine("    FONT-SIZE: 10px;")
txtstream.WriteLine("    text-align: left;")
txtstream.WriteLine("    white-Space: nowrap='nowrap';")
txtstream.WriteLine("    width: 100%;")
txtstream.WriteLine("}")
txtstream.WriteLine("input")
txtstream.WriteLine("{")
txtstream.WriteLine("    COLOR: black;")
txtstream.WriteLine("    BACKGROUND-COLOR: white;")
txtstream.WriteLine("    FONT-FAMILY: font-family: Cambria, serif;")
txtstream.WriteLine("    FONT-SIZE: 12px;")
txtstream.WriteLine("    text-align: left;")
txtstream.WriteLine("    display:table-cell;")
```

```
txtstream.WriteLine("    white-Space: nowrap='nowrap';")
txtstream.WriteLine("}")
txtstream.WriteLine("h1 {")
txtstream.WriteLine("color: antiquewhite;")
txtstream.WriteLine("text-shadow: 1px 1px 1px black;")
txtstream.WriteLine("padding: 3px;")
txtstream.WriteLine("text-align: center;")
txtstream.WriteLine("box-shadow: in2px 2px 5px rgba(0,0,0,0.5), in-2px -
2px 5px rgba(255,255,255,0.5);")
txtstream.WriteLine("}")
txtstream.WriteLine("</style>")
```

```
txtstream.WriteLine("<style type='text/css'>")
txtstream.WriteLine("body")
txtstream.WriteLine("{")
txtstream.WriteLine("    PADDING-RIGHT: 0px;")
txtstream.WriteLine("    PADDING-LEFT: 0px;")
txtstream.WriteLine("    PADDING-BOTTOM: 0px;")
txtstream.WriteLine("    MARGIN: 0px;")
txtstream.WriteLine("    COLOR: #333;")
txtstream.WriteLine("    PADDING-TOP: 0px;")
txtstream.WriteLine("    FONT-FAMILY: verdana, arial, helvetica, sans-serif;")
txtstream.WriteLine("}")
txtstream.WriteLine("table")
txtstream.WriteLine("{")
txtstream.WriteLine("    BORDER-RIGHT: #999999 3px solid;")
txtstream.WriteLine("    PADDING-RIGHT: 6px;")
txtstream.WriteLine("    PADDING-LEFT: 6px;")
txtstream.WriteLine("    FONT-WEIGHT: Bold;")
txtstream.WriteLine("    FONT-SIZE: 14px;")
txtstream.WriteLine("    PADDING-BOTTOM: 6px;")
txtstream.WriteLine("    COLOR: Peru;")
txtstream.WriteLine("    LINE-HEIGHT: 14px;")
txtstream.WriteLine("    PADDING-TOP: 6px;")
txtstream.WriteLine("    BORDER-BOTTOM: #999 1px solid;")
txtstream.WriteLine("    BACKGROUND-COLOR: #eeeeee;")
```

```
txtstream.WriteLine("   FONT-FAMILY: verdana, arial, helvetica, sans-serif;")
txtstream.WriteLine("   FONT-SIZE: 12px;")
txtstream.WriteLine("}")
txtstream.WriteLine("th")
txtstream.WriteLine("{")
txtstream.WriteLine("   BORDER-RIGHT: #999999 3px solid;")
txtstream.WriteLine("   PADDING-RIGHT: 6px;")
txtstream.WriteLine("   PADDING-LEFT: 6px;")
txtstream.WriteLine("   FONT-WEIGHT: Bold;")
txtstream.WriteLine("   FONT-SIZE: 14px;")
txtstream.WriteLine("   PADDING-BOTTOM: 6px;")
txtstream.WriteLine("   COLOR: darkred;")
txtstream.WriteLine("   LINE-HEIGHT: 14px;")
txtstream.WriteLine("   PADDING-TOP: 6px;")
txtstream.WriteLine("   BORDER-BOTTOM: #999 1px solid;")
txtstream.WriteLine("   BACKGROUND-COLOR: #eeeeee;")
txtstream.WriteLine("   FONT-FAMILY: Cambria, serif;")
txtstream.WriteLine("   FONT-SIZE: 12px;")
txtstream.WriteLine("   text-align: left;")
txtstream.WriteLine("   white-Space: nowrap='nowrap';")
txtstream.WriteLine("}")
txtstream.WriteLine(".th")
txtstream.WriteLine("{")
txtstream.WriteLine("   BORDER-RIGHT: #999999 2px solid;")
txtstream.WriteLine("   PADDING-RIGHT: 6px;")
txtstream.WriteLine("   PADDING-LEFT: 6px;")
txtstream.WriteLine("   FONT-WEIGHT: Bold;")
txtstream.WriteLine("   PADDING-BOTTOM: 6px;")
txtstream.WriteLine("   COLOR: black;")
txtstream.WriteLine("   PADDING-TOP: 6px;")
txtstream.WriteLine("   BORDER-BOTTOM: #999 2px solid;")
txtstream.WriteLine("   BACKGROUND-COLOR: #eeeeee;")
txtstream.WriteLine("   FONT-FAMILY: font-family: Cambria, serif;")
txtstream.WriteLine("   FONT-SIZE: 10px;")
txtstream.WriteLine("   text-align: right;")
txtstream.WriteLine("   white-Space: nowrap='nowrap';")
txtstream.WriteLine("}")
txtstream.WriteLine("td")
txtstream.WriteLine("{")
txtstream.WriteLine("   BORDER-RIGHT: #999999 3px solid;")
```

```
txtstream.WriteLine("    PADDING-RIGHT: 6px;")
txtstream.WriteLine("    PADDING-LEFT: 6px;")
txtstream.WriteLine("    FONT-WEIGHT: Normal;")
txtstream.WriteLine("    PADDING-BOTTOM: 6px;")
txtstream.WriteLine("    COLOR: navy;")
txtstream.WriteLine("    LINE-HEIGHT: 14px;")
txtstream.WriteLine("    PADDING-TOP: 6px;")
txtstream.WriteLine("    BORDER-BOTTOM: #999 1px solid;")
txtstream.WriteLine("    BACKGROUND-COLOR: #eeeeee;")
txtstream.WriteLine("    FONT-FAMILY: font-family: Cambria, serif;")
txtstream.WriteLine("    FONT-SIZE: 12px;")
txtstream.WriteLine("    text-align: left;")
txtstream.WriteLine("    white-Space: nowrap='nowrap';")
txtstream.WriteLine("}")
txtstream.WriteLine("div")
txtstream.WriteLine("{")
txtstream.WriteLine("    BORDER-RIGHT: #999999 3px solid;")
txtstream.WriteLine("    PADDING-RIGHT: 6px;")
txtstream.WriteLine("    PADDING-LEFT: 6px;")
txtstream.WriteLine("    FONT-WEIGHT: Normal;")
txtstream.WriteLine("    PADDING-BOTTOM: 6px;")
txtstream.WriteLine("    COLOR: white;")
txtstream.WriteLine("    PADDING-TOP: 6px;")
txtstream.WriteLine("    BORDER-BOTTOM: #999 1px solid;")
txtstream.WriteLine("    BACKGROUND-COLOR: navy;")
txtstream.WriteLine("    FONT-FAMILY: font-family: Cambria, serif;")
txtstream.WriteLine("    FONT-SIZE: 10px;")
txtstream.WriteLine("    text-align: left;")
txtstream.WriteLine("    white-Space: nowrap='nowrap';")
txtstream.WriteLine("}")
txtstream.WriteLine("span")
txtstream.WriteLine("{")
txtstream.WriteLine("    BORDER-RIGHT: #999999 3px solid;")
txtstream.WriteLine("    PADDING-RIGHT: 3px;")
txtstream.WriteLine("    PADDING-LEFT: 3px;")
txtstream.WriteLine("    FONT-WEIGHT: Normal;")
txtstream.WriteLine("    PADDING-BOTTOM: 3px;")
txtstream.WriteLine("    COLOR: white;")
txtstream.WriteLine("    PADDING-TOP: 3px;")
txtstream.WriteLine("    BORDER-BOTTOM: #999 1px solid;")
```

```
txtstream.WriteLine("    BACKGROUND-COLOR: navy;")
txtstream.WriteLine("    FONT-FAMILY: font-family: Cambria, serif;")
txtstream.WriteLine("    FONT-SIZE: 10px;")
txtstream.WriteLine("    text-align: left;")
txtstream.WriteLine("    white-Space: nowrap='nowrap';")
txtstream.WriteLine("    display:inline-block;")
txtstream.WriteLine("    width: 100%;")
txtstream.WriteLine("}")
txtstream.WriteLine("textarea")
txtstream.WriteLine("{")
txtstream.WriteLine("    BORDER-RIGHT: #999999 3px solid;")
txtstream.WriteLine("    PADDING-RIGHT: 3px;")
txtstream.WriteLine("    PADDING-LEFT: 3px;")
txtstream.WriteLine("    FONT-WEIGHT: Normal;")
txtstream.WriteLine("    PADDING-BOTTOM: 3px;")
txtstream.WriteLine("    COLOR: white;")
txtstream.WriteLine("    PADDING-TOP: 3px;")
txtstream.WriteLine("    BORDER-BOTTOM: #999 1px solid;")
txtstream.WriteLine("    BACKGROUND-COLOR: navy;")
txtstream.WriteLine("    FONT-FAMILY: font-family: Cambria, serif;")
txtstream.WriteLine("    FONT-SIZE: 10px;")
txtstream.WriteLine("    text-align: left;")
txtstream.WriteLine("    white-Space: nowrap='nowrap';")
txtstream.WriteLine("    width: 100%;")
txtstream.WriteLine("}")
txtstream.WriteLine("select")
txtstream.WriteLine("{")
txtstream.WriteLine("    BORDER-RIGHT: #999999 3px solid;")
txtstream.WriteLine("    PADDING-RIGHT: 6px;")
txtstream.WriteLine("    PADDING-LEFT: 6px;")
txtstream.WriteLine("    FONT-WEIGHT: Normal;")
txtstream.WriteLine("    PADDING-BOTTOM: 6px;")
txtstream.WriteLine("    COLOR: white;")
txtstream.WriteLine("    PADDING-TOP: 6px;")
txtstream.WriteLine("    BORDER-BOTTOM: #999 1px solid;")
txtstream.WriteLine("    BACKGROUND-COLOR: navy;")
txtstream.WriteLine("    FONT-FAMILY: font-family: Cambria, serif;")
txtstream.WriteLine("    FONT-SIZE: 10px;")
txtstream.WriteLine("    text-align: left;")
txtstream.WriteLine("    white-Space: nowrap='nowrap';")
```

```
txtstream.WriteLine("    width: 100%;")
txtstream.WriteLine("}")
txtstream.WriteLine("input")
txtstream.WriteLine("{")
txtstream.WriteLine("    BORDER-RIGHT: #999999 3px solid;")
txtstream.WriteLine("    PADDING-RIGHT: 3px;")
txtstream.WriteLine("    PADDING-LEFT: 3px;")
txtstream.WriteLine("    FONT-WEIGHT: Bold;")
txtstream.WriteLine("    PADDING-BOTTOM: 3px;")
txtstream.WriteLine("    COLOR: white;")
txtstream.WriteLine("    PADDING-TOP: 3px;")
txtstream.WriteLine("    BORDER-BOTTOM: #999 1px solid;")
txtstream.WriteLine("    BACKGROUND-COLOR: navy;")
txtstream.WriteLine("    FONT-FAMILY: font-family: Cambria, serif;")
txtstream.WriteLine("    FONT-SIZE: 12px;")
txtstream.WriteLine("    text-align: left;")
txtstream.WriteLine("    display:table-cell;")
txtstream.WriteLine("    white-Space: nowrap='nowrap';")
txtstream.WriteLine("    width: 100%;")
txtstream.WriteLine("}")
txtstream.WriteLine("h1 {")
txtstream.WriteLine("color: antiquewhite;")
txtstream.WriteLine("text-shadow: 1px 1px 1px black;")
txtstream.WriteLine("padding: 3px;")
txtstream.WriteLine("text-align: center;")
txtstream.WriteLine("box-shadow: in2px 2px 5px rgba(0,0,0,0.5), in-2px -2px 5px rgba(255,255,255,0.5);")
txtstream.WriteLine("}")
txtstream.WriteLine("</style>")
```

SHADOW BOX

```
txtstream.WriteLine("<style type='text/css'>")
txtstream.WriteLine("body")
txtstream.WriteLine("{")
txtstream.WriteLine("    PADDING-RIGHT: 0px;")
txtstream.WriteLine("    PADDING-LEFT: 0px;")
txtstream.WriteLine("    PADDING-BOTTOM: 0px;")
```

```
txtstream.WriteLine("    MARGIN: 0px;")
txtstream.WriteLine("    COLOR: #333;")
txtstream.WriteLine("    PADDING-TOP: 0px;")
txtstream.WriteLine("    FONT-FAMILY: verdana, arial, helvetica, sans-serif;")
txtstream.WriteLine("}")
txtstream.WriteLine("table")
txtstream.WriteLine("{")
txtstream.WriteLine("    BORDER-RIGHT: #999999 1px solid;")
txtstream.WriteLine("    PADDING-RIGHT: 1px;")
txtstream.WriteLine("    PADDING-LEFT: 1px;")
txtstream.WriteLine("    PADDING-BOTTOM: 1px;")
txtstream.WriteLine("    LINE-HEIGHT: 8px;")
txtstream.WriteLine("    PADDING-TOP: 1px;")
txtstream.WriteLine("    BORDER-BOTTOM: #999 1px solid;")
txtstream.WriteLine("    BACKGROUND-COLOR: #eeeeee;")
txtstream.WriteLine("
filter:progid:DXImageTransform.Microsoft.Shadow(color='silver',    Direction=135,
Strength=16)")
txtstream.WriteLine("}")
txtstream.WriteLine("th")
txtstream.WriteLine("{")
txtstream.WriteLine("    BORDER-RIGHT: #999999 3px solid;")
txtstream.WriteLine("    PADDING-RIGHT: 6px;")
txtstream.WriteLine("    PADDING-LEFT: 6px;")
txtstream.WriteLine("    FONT-WEIGHT: Bold;")
txtstream.WriteLine("    FONT-SIZE: 14px;")
txtstream.WriteLine("    PADDING-BOTTOM: 6px;")
txtstream.WriteLine("    COLOR: darkred;")
txtstream.WriteLine("    LINE-HEIGHT: 14px;")
txtstream.WriteLine("    PADDING-TOP: 6px;")
txtstream.WriteLine("    BORDER-BOTTOM: #999 1px solid;")
txtstream.WriteLine("    BACKGROUND-COLOR: #eeeeee;")
txtstream.WriteLine("    FONT-FAMILY: font-family: Cambria, serif;")
txtstream.WriteLine("    FONT-SIZE: 12px;")
txtstream.WriteLine("    text-align: left;")
txtstream.WriteLine("    white-Space: nowrap='nowrap';")
txtstream.WriteLine("}")
txtstream.WriteLine(".th")
txtstream.WriteLine("{")
txtstream.WriteLine("    BORDER-RIGHT: #999999 2px solid;")
```

```
txtstream.WriteLine("    PADDING-RIGHT: 6px;")
txtstream.WriteLine("    PADDING-LEFT: 6px;")
txtstream.WriteLine("    FONT-WEIGHT: Bold;")
txtstream.WriteLine("    PADDING-BOTTOM: 6px;")
txtstream.WriteLine("    COLOR: black;")
txtstream.WriteLine("    PADDING-TOP: 6px;")
txtstream.WriteLine("    BORDER-BOTTOM: #999 2px solid;")
txtstream.WriteLine("    BACKGROUND-COLOR: #eeeeee;")
txtstream.WriteLine("    FONT-FAMILY: font-family: Cambria, serif;")
txtstream.WriteLine("    FONT-SIZE: 10px;")
txtstream.WriteLine("    text-align: right;")
txtstream.WriteLine("    white-Space: nowrap='nowrap';")
txtstream.WriteLine("}")
txtstream.WriteLine("td")
txtstream.WriteLine("{")
txtstream.WriteLine("    BORDER-RIGHT: #999999 3px solid;")
txtstream.WriteLine("    PADDING-RIGHT: 6px;")
txtstream.WriteLine("    PADDING-LEFT: 6px;")
txtstream.WriteLine("    FONT-WEIGHT: Normal;")
txtstream.WriteLine("    PADDING-BOTTOM: 6px;")
txtstream.WriteLine("    COLOR: navy;")
txtstream.WriteLine("    LINE-HEIGHT: 14px;")
txtstream.WriteLine("    PADDING-TOP: 6px;")
txtstream.WriteLine("    BORDER-BOTTOM: #999 1px solid;")
txtstream.WriteLine("    BACKGROUND-COLOR: #eeeeee;")
txtstream.WriteLine("    FONT-FAMILY: font-family: Cambria, serif;")
txtstream.WriteLine("    FONT-SIZE: 12px;")
txtstream.WriteLine("    text-align: left;")
txtstream.WriteLine("    white-Space: nowrap='nowrap';")
txtstream.WriteLine("}")
txtstream.WriteLine("div")
txtstream.WriteLine("{")
txtstream.WriteLine("    BORDER-RIGHT: #999999 3px solid;")
txtstream.WriteLine("    PADDING-RIGHT: 6px;")
txtstream.WriteLine("    PADDING-LEFT: 6px;")
txtstream.WriteLine("    FONT-WEIGHT: Normal;")
txtstream.WriteLine("    PADDING-BOTTOM: 6px;")
txtstream.WriteLine("    COLOR: white;")
txtstream.WriteLine("    PADDING-TOP: 6px;")
txtstream.WriteLine("    BORDER-BOTTOM: #999 1px solid;")
```

```
txtstream.WriteLine("    BACKGROUND-COLOR: navy;")
txtstream.WriteLine("    FONT-FAMILY: font-family: Cambria, serif;")
txtstream.WriteLine("    FONT-SIZE: 10px;")
txtstream.WriteLine("    text-align: left;")
txtstream.WriteLine("    white-Space: nowrap='nowrap';")
txtstream.WriteLine("}")
txtstream.WriteLine("span")
txtstream.WriteLine("{")
txtstream.WriteLine("    BORDER-RIGHT: #999999 3px solid;")
txtstream.WriteLine("    PADDING-RIGHT: 3px;")
txtstream.WriteLine("    PADDING-LEFT: 3px;")
txtstream.WriteLine("    FONT-WEIGHT: Normal;")
txtstream.WriteLine("    PADDING-BOTTOM: 3px;")
txtstream.WriteLine("    COLOR: white;")
txtstream.WriteLine("    PADDING-TOP: 3px;")
txtstream.WriteLine("    BORDER-BOTTOM: #999 1px solid;")
txtstream.WriteLine("    BACKGROUND-COLOR: navy;")
txtstream.WriteLine("    FONT-FAMILY: font-family: Cambria, serif;")
txtstream.WriteLine("    FONT-SIZE: 10px;")
txtstream.WriteLine("    text-align: left;")
txtstream.WriteLine("    white-Space: nowrap='nowrap';")
txtstream.WriteLine("    display: inline-block;")
txtstream.WriteLine("    width: 100%;")
txtstream.WriteLine("}")
txtstream.WriteLine("textarea")
txtstream.WriteLine("{")
txtstream.WriteLine("    BORDER-RIGHT: #999999 3px solid;")
txtstream.WriteLine("    PADDING-RIGHT: 3px;")
txtstream.WriteLine("    PADDING-LEFT: 3px;")
txtstream.WriteLine("    FONT-WEIGHT: Normal;")
txtstream.WriteLine("    PADDING-BOTTOM: 3px;")
txtstream.WriteLine("    COLOR: white;")
txtstream.WriteLine("    PADDING-TOP: 3px;")
txtstream.WriteLine("    BORDER-BOTTOM: #999 1px solid;")
txtstream.WriteLine("    BACKGROUND-COLOR: navy;")
txtstream.WriteLine("    FONT-FAMILY: font-family: Cambria, serif;")
txtstream.WriteLine("    FONT-SIZE: 10px;")
txtstream.WriteLine("    text-align: left;")
txtstream.WriteLine("    white-Space: nowrap='nowrap';")
txtstream.WriteLine("    width: 100%;")
```

```
txtstream.WriteLine("}")
txtstream.WriteLine("select")
txtstream.WriteLine("{")
txtstream.WriteLine("   BORDER-RIGHT: #999999 3px solid;")
txtstream.WriteLine("   PADDING-RIGHT: 6px;")
txtstream.WriteLine("   PADDING-LEFT: 6px;")
txtstream.WriteLine("   FONT-WEIGHT: Normal;")
txtstream.WriteLine("   PADDING-BOTTOM: 6px;")
txtstream.WriteLine("   COLOR: white;")
txtstream.WriteLine("   PADDING-TOP: 6px;")
txtstream.WriteLine("   BORDER-BOTTOM: #999 1px solid;")
txtstream.WriteLine("   BACKGROUND-COLOR: navy;")
txtstream.WriteLine("   FONT-FAMILY: font-family: Cambria, serif;")
txtstream.WriteLine("   FONT-SIZE: 10px;")
txtstream.WriteLine("   text-align: left;")
txtstream.WriteLine("   white-Space: nowrap='nowrap';")
txtstream.WriteLine("   width: 100%;")
txtstream.WriteLine("}")
txtstream.WriteLine("input")
txtstream.WriteLine("{")
txtstream.WriteLine("   BORDER-RIGHT: #999999 3px solid;")
txtstream.WriteLine("   PADDING-RIGHT: 3px;")
txtstream.WriteLine("   PADDING-LEFT: 3px;")
txtstream.WriteLine("   FONT-WEIGHT: Bold;")
txtstream.WriteLine("   PADDING-BOTTOM: 3px;")
txtstream.WriteLine("   COLOR: white;")
txtstream.WriteLine("   PADDING-TOP: 3px;")
txtstream.WriteLine("   BORDER-BOTTOM: #999 1px solid;")
txtstream.WriteLine("   BACKGROUND-COLOR: navy;")
txtstream.WriteLine("   FONT-FAMILY: font-family: Cambria, serif;")
txtstream.WriteLine("   FONT-SIZE: 12px;")
txtstream.WriteLine("   text-align: left;")
txtstream.WriteLine("   display: table-cell;")
txtstream.WriteLine("   white-Space: nowrap='nowrap';")
txtstream.WriteLine("   width: 100%;")
txtstream.WriteLine("}")
txtstream.WriteLine("h1 {")
txtstream.WriteLine("color: antiquewhite;")
txtstream.WriteLine("text-shadow: 1px 1px 1px black;")
txtstream.WriteLine("padding: 3px;")
```

```
txtstream.WriteLine("text-align: center;")
txtstream.WriteLine("box-shadow: in2px 2px 5px rgba(0,0,0,0.5), in-2px -
2px 5px rgba(255,255,255,0.5);")
txtstream.WriteLine("}")
txtstream.WriteLine("</style>")
```